INDEX ON CENSORSHIP

INDEX ON CENSORSHIP 5 2000

INDEX ON CENSORSHIP

Volume 29 No 5 September/October 2000 Issue 196

WEBSITE NEWS UPDATED WEEKLY

www.indexoncensorship.org
contact@indexoncensorship.org
tel: **020 7278 2313**
fax: **020 7278 1878**

Index on Censorship (ISSN 0306-4220) is published bi-monthly by a non-profit-making company: Writers & Scholars International Ltd, Lancaster House, 33 Islington High Street, London N1 9LH. *Index on Censorship* is associated with Writers & Scholars Educational Trust, registered charity number 325003
Periodicals postage: (US subscribers only) paid at Newark, New Jersey.
Postmaster: send US address changes to *Index on Censorship* c/o Mercury Airfreight International Ltd Inc, 365 Blair Road, Avenel, NJ 07001, USA

Subscriptions (6 issues per annum)
Individuals: Britain £39, US $52, rest of world £45
Institutions: Britain £44, US $80, rest of world £50
Speak to Tony Callaghan on 020 7278 2313
or email tony@indexoncensorship.org

EDITORIAL

If in doubt, cut it out

There are two questions uppermost in the minds of 16 million Muscovites: should they abolish August, as intimated by *Moskovski Novosti* (Moscow News) in its front page; and what on earth to do with no television. 'The strange fatalities of August' started back in 1991, reminded a local radio station. They resumed with the financial meltdown of 1998; continued in 1999 with the war in Daghestan and the political crisis in the Kremlin; and culminated in August 2000's grand slam. It began with the bomb in the Pushkin Square underpass on 8 August (12 dead); continued with the prolonged tragedy of the submarine Kursk (12 August, 118 dead); and ended with the fire in the Ostankino TV tower (27 August, 'only' four dead, but the loss of all those familiar friends in Ostankino soaps, dead for several months at least, loudly mourned).

Psychologists predict acute distress among the elderly and retired, a surfeit of sex among the young; the police fear an explosion of drugs and 'crimes of boredom'; and the emergency medical services report an abnormally large number of distress calls, particularly heart attacks. On the bright side, newspaper sales have gone up by 50% and news sites on the Internet have a new lease of life.

But the really good news this black August is the ferocity with which the Russians let their leaders know, in the wake of the Kursk disaster, they will be lied to no longer, the clearest sign yet of the development of a civil society from the bottom up.

'What do you mean by censorship?' they asked me at a conference for journalists in Estonia a couple of weeks ago. Strange question in that part of the world, for so long synonymous with the term. 'We don't have that any more.' So we put up a free microphone in the town's main square and encouraged the citizen's of Pärnu to come up and speak their mind. It took two days for people to give voice. Then they talked of inaccessible local representatives who ignored their voice once elected; of the media silence that hid the rebirth of TB; of the poverty and humiliation of ethnic Russians, still second-class subjects – not citizens – of this urbane nation. Our journalists began to see that 'censorship', as we try to show in our post-communist *Index*, is a much more nuanced matter than their 'only state repression'. Who would have thought that in Estonia, as in Russia, it's the simple folk who eventually tell it like it is.

But things are always so different 'in there' from what we are told 'back here'. ❏

contents

What! You who are evil,
Ugly and uncivil.
You who are cruel...

Yes, you must bless us.

But the evil you do,
The endless ado.
Why bless you?...

With Israel's withdrawal, Lebanon stands at the crossroads, in danger of the peace that may break out at any moment

news in the

● **Lords a-leaping** On 14 June, a troupe of traditional Morris dancers were stopped from performing at a multi-cultural festival in Carlisle, Cumbria, when council officials thought their black and white face masks were 'racist'. The players were finally allowed to participate after they explained that their blacked-up faces represented medieval poachers' disguise. In London, meanwhile, moves were afoot to lift a 200-year-old law banning sitting Lords from dancing on the Sabbath. John Grogan, Labour MP for Selby, pointed out that, regardless of the law, most Lords were disinclined to move on a Sunday, let alone groove.

● **Bloomtunes blanked** Stephen Joyce, grandson of author James Joyce and a curator of the writer's estate, has instructed an amateur theatre company to cancel plans to stage a musical adaptation of the final chapter of *Ulysses*, due to be staged at August's Edinburgh Fringe Festival. Joyce accused the play, which contains one song titled 'Rap of Spunk', and another named 'Song of Sucking', of turning a 'masterful work' into a 'circus act'. Stephen Joyce is well known for his protective approach to his illustrious ancestor's work. This magazine was warned on one occasion: 'If you quote a single word, I'll send in the tanks'.

● **Cock and bull** When US attorney Sherril Babcock attempted to register at BlackPlanet.com in mid-August, she received a message saying the website could not accept her application unless she changed her name. On querying web manager Crystal Martin, Babcock learned that the site's censorship software deemed 'the letters that form the word "cock" unacceptable'. Martin said the filtering programme could not be disengaged, and that a name-change was unavoidable. This is not the first occasion that Internet censors have come a cropper. Last year American Online banned the use of 'breast' in its chatrooms, leaving visitors to a breast cancer forum with little to discuss.

● **Nasty habits** Orthodox monks have ditched Byzantine chants for hardcore anthems after recording a CD that reached ethereal heights in the Greek hit parade in June. Breaking a thousand years of tradition, the walls of the Saints Augustine and Seraphim Sarof monastery now reverberate to beats from a black-robed posse. 'Guns, drugs, showbiz, money, political backstage … don't just talk about revolution…', goes the single 'Anarchy and Rock'. The monks, aged 18 to 30, say they just 'want to reach out to the masses'.

● **Abusers' guides** The Romanian edition of *Playboy* caused a stir among its US corporate bosses with a recent article, entitled 'How to beat your wife without leaving marks'. Pictures of domestic violence accompanied the piece, which *Playboy* in the US disavowed. Not to be outdone, a state-funded religious foundation in Turkey has published a volume, the *Muslim's Handbook*, that says men may beat their wives as long as they 'avoid the face' and do not strike 'too hard'. The book advises men to take a second wife if the first is ill, or the man is too poor to afford a servant.

● **Buying silence** Fourth Estate, the independent book publisher set up in 1984, finally fell to Rupert Murdoch's empire over the summer when Guardian Media Group sold its controlling share to News International's HarperCollins. One of the first victims is Michael Crick's unauthorised biography of Murdoch himself. Crick found fame with his exposé of disgraced Tory politician, Lord Jeffery Archer. Two years ago, when News International bought HarperCollins, plans to publish Chris Patten's book about Hong Kong, *East and West*, were dropped, allegedly because it threatened Murdoch's Chinese interests (*Index* 3/1998).

● **Billion-dollar bottle** Intellect, a Russian investment company now owns the patent on the humble bottle. In principle, everyone, from beer, wine and soft-drink manufacturers to artists producing an artefact loosely resembling the well-known container, is legally required to pass on 0.5 % of their total profits to the mysterious owners of Intellect. The company, which has also patented the railroad, is running rings around Russia's fledgling patent laws.

● **Cabin fever** Ten 'foreigners' were locked inside a portable office block in the centre of Vienna by German theatre director Christoph Schlingenseif on 11 June. Every day, 'voters' were asked to choose which one should be 'deported'. Votes could be cast by telephone or over the Internet and a sign was hung outside the block with the words 'Foreigners Out'. The event, entitled *Please Love Austria*, was designed as a hybrid between the popular TV show *Big Brother*, currently hypnotising spectators from Germany to the US, and the anti-immigration policies espoused by Austria's Freedom party. The right-wing party threatened to sue Schlingenseif for using its symbols and, on 15 June, part of the set was torched in an arson attack.

● **Short shrift** In sharp contrast to Iran's lowering press climate, the state eased the dress code in July, allowing schoolgirls to bin their blue, brown and black drab and don 'bright, happy colours' in class. 'Light blue, beige, pink, light green and yellow' all appear on the official list of approved colours. On the same day in Swaziland, the government banned miniskirts in school in a bid to halt sexual liaisons between teachers and pupils in a country where 25% of the population is HIV positive. Meanwhile, Afghanistan's Olympic hopes suffered a body blow when Taliban guards detained 12 members of a visiting Pakistani football squad, as they limbered up before spectators in Kandahar stadium in July. The players had broken local *sharia* laws by doffing the long, baggy *shalwar kameez* in favour of shorts. Their heads were shaved and they were deported.

● **Gel smell hell** A 17-year-old schoolboy was arrested in June and suspended from school in Halifax, Canada, for flouting a law that bans the wearing in public of colognes, perfumes and fragrances. The boy was reported by a teacher who complained of feeling sick after inhaling Gary Falkenham's Dippity-Do hair gel and underarm deodorant. The town, which has introduced a 'no-scent encouragement programme', is periodically flooded with surgically-masked scientists monitoring 'artificial odour levels' in a seaport where the smell of freshly landed fish jostles with the odour of human sweat.

● **Capital sin** Anya Provorova, a 17-year-old schoolgirl in a village north of Moscow, was stripped of her diploma and lost her place at a medical school after writing a letter asking President Valdimir Putin for a video camera to record her graduation ceremony. In her salutation to 'Esteemed Vladimir Vladimirovich Putin', it seems Provorova missed out the customary exclamation mark and, when using the Russian word for 'you', she omitted a capital letter. Her grades were lowered as a punishment, though her marks had already been published. The four-page report from the local authority revising her results contained 33 spelling mistakes, 97 punctuation errors ... and two solecisms.

● **Flash phobia** From Prince William to baby Leo Blair, British royalty and politicians have been exerting pressure on editors and broadcasters to leave their children in peace. Protection of privacy for 18-year-old William, legally an adult, was assured after lengthy chats between Buckingham Palace and the Press Complaints Commission. Similarly, the Blair family negotiated a deal, exchanging an official holiday photo call in Tuscany for the promise of an intrusion-free vacation. But while the PM's baby and the royal family's offspring are off-limits, other rich kids are considered fair game. Posh Spice Victoria Beckham wanted to know why special exceptions are made for Will and Leo, when baby Brooklyn gets flash phobia every time he's taken out.

● **Caustic comment** A German anti-abortion group that coined the slogan 'Babycaust', likening the 'murder of children in their mothers' wombs' to the Holocaust, won a legal battle in June to let them use the word. The authorities at a Nuremburg hospital had succeeded in obtaining an injunction ordering the group to refrain from using such 'inflammatory language', but a Munich court overturned the ruling. It said that the campaigners had not acted 'mendaciously' by declaring abortion to be a 'mass extermination of life'. Feminist groups berated the court for its decision. Anja Klauk of the German Feminist Party protested: 'This verdict brands women as murderers.'

● **NATO in the dock** The traditional status of the media as a civilian, rather than military, target was reinforced in a 13 June report by the International Criminal Tribunal for Former Yugoslavia (ICTFY). It was investigating war crimes committed against Serbs during the 1999 NATO bombing campaign. Allied air strikes, from 24 March to 10 June, killed up to 600 civilians and damaged thousands of buildings. Among them was the Belgrade headquarters of Serbian state radio and television (RTS), bombed on 23 April.

The ICTFY condemned the bombing, in which 16 members of staff were killed, but declared that media outlets could justifiably be identified as military targets in certain circumstances. 'If the media is used to incite crimes, as in Rwanda, or is the nerve system that keeps a warmonger in power', it would forfeit its civilian status, the Tribunal observed.

The ICTFY deemed that the NATO attack on RTS contravened Protocol I of the Geneva Convention. This states: 'Civilians shall enjoy the protection [from military attack] unless, and for such time as, they take a *direct* part in hostilities.' And it dismissed a claim on 8 June by General Wesley Clark, Supreme Allied Commander of NATO, that because RTS 'exported fear, hatred and instability into neighbouring regions', it was a legitimate target of war. The report said that the dissemination of propaganda designed to 'foster support for the war effort' did not render a media organisation's immunity from attack forfeit.

The Tribunal heard that NATO commanders, incensed by RTS coverage of allied aircraft strafing civilians, identified the organisation's headquarters as a target. It suggested NATO violated international law by 'deliberately directing attacks against civilian objects' and 'failing to provide advanced warning' of its intentions. The tribunal concluded that these actions were war crimes.

Despite its findings, however, the ICTFY said that no criminal investigation against NATO could be launched. 'Either the law is not sufficiently clear,' it concluded, 'or investigations are unlikely to result in the acquisition of sufficient evidence to substantiate charges against high-level accused, or against lower accused for particularly heinous offences.'

David Gelber

● **Meet the new boss** Away from the choreographed party

conventions, where even the ad-libs are tele-prompted, Americans might be forgiven for wondering where the differences lie between presidential front-runners George W Bush and Al Gore. Not on foreign policy, the war on drugs and military expansion – Gore and Bush differ only on their scheduling of the globally destabilising National Missile Defence scheme. When confronted with such lacklustre candidates it's hard to accept the premise that personality has replaced policy, but it is difficult to slip a cigarette paper between the two on 'mainstream' issues. What, then, of censorship?

Favoured Son, an unauthorised biography of Bush, revealed the measures taken by George Sr to keep his boy out of Vietnam, and detailed decades of drug abuse – making great sport of Bush's hypocritical anti-cocaine legislation as governor of Texas. Despite high sales, *Favoured Son's* publishers mysteriously pulped the book. Bush then turned to the Internet, threatening legal action before buying up hundreds of 'defamatory' domain names – tap in *www.georgebushsucks.com* and the official George Bush for President site loads. Back in Texas, Bush passed a bill forbidding state investment in any company that

'writes, records, produces, advertises, markets, sells, or otherwise promotes any song, lyrics, or other musical works' deemed offensive.

However, it is in the Democrat camp that censorship finds its real home. Gore's running mate, Joe Lieberman, founded the Silver Sewer Awards. Justifying the mock awards, principally directed at Hollywood, Lieberman said: 'it was our intention to dishonour leading cultural polluters'. In 1985 Tipper Gore founded the Parents Music Resource Centre. Responsible for stickering countless albums with 'Parental Guidance: Explicit Lyrics' tags, the PMRC was denounced by, among others, Frank Zappa: 'People who write bad laws are in my opinion more dangerous than songwriters who celebrate sexuality.'

As vice-president, Al Gore ordered industry to develop Internet filtering systems. He also launched initiatives to make the censoring 'V Chip' mandatory in all new TV sets. Now Gore is playing censorship as a vote-winner: 'Parents deserve more control over the violence and degradation peddled to their children as entertainment. Twenty years ago, Tipper was right.' ❑

FF

●**Mumbo gumbo** Cookery programmes, travel shows and children's TV represent the reality of life in developing countries far more accurately than most news and current affairs coverage, says a report by the Glasgow Media Group (GMG), published on 28 July. It reveals how the information on the outside world the British get from TV – their main source of this sort of information – is skewed and inaccurate. 'The most positive and well-explained coverage was on the BBC's children's news programme *Newsround*, and in documentaries,' the report concludes. 'Other positive images came from cookery and wildlife programmes, and from innovative documentaries.' Singled out for special praise were BBC2 cookery shows, *Rick Stein's Seafood Odyssey* and *Ainsley's Big Cook-out* – 'effectively a celebration of South American culture, including comments on the history and ecology of the country featured.'

Viewing the World was commissioned by the Department For International Development as part of its mandate to raise public understanding of development issues. Examining the kinds of images British viewers were being offered and how TV decision-makers approach their global content, the report identified 'a marked imbalance in the way developing countries are portrayed, especially on news where coverage was generally limited to disasters, bizarre events or visits by prominent westerners'.

Attempts by NGOs to gain media attention with visiting celebs may well backfire, the report suggests, as TV tends to dwell on the antics of the enlisted footballers and pop stars, rather than highlight the intended issues. The Spice Girls cavorting with Mandela makes good viewing, but hardly explains the complexities of post-apartheid South Africa.

An audience survey found TV a strong source of beliefs and impressions about the developing world. 'Viewers generally perceived the world in a negative way, blaming this on TV images.' The study also highlighted the dilemma facing producers: 'Policy-makers all recognise the importance of TV's role in informing people about the world, but most doubt that viewers want to watch programmes about the developing world, so this output has come to be regarded as a ratings risk.'

Peter Moszynski

TOM FAWTHROP

Dili dallying

Of the funds so far allocated for the reconstruction of East Timor, only US$59 million have been used for that purpose. US$680 million have been spent on UN peacekeeping, policing and relief operations, or gone into the pockets of the UN's legion of foreign contractors

A looming symbol of the UN presence in East Timor, the 500-room Olympia, a floating hotel chartered for its personnel when the UN established its presence here exactly one year ago, blots out the sunset over the Dili waterfront. Like every other structure in the capital, hotels were destroyed during Operation Clean Sweep, the 16-day reign of terror dreamed up by the Indonesian military to avenge the loss of its 27th province when the East Timorese voted for independence on 30 August 1999. Between 4 and 20 September, Indonesian-backed militias gutted more than 80,000 buildings, killed 600 people and forced 80% of the population into the mountains, or across the border to live as virtual hostages in 250 Indonesian 'refugee' camps.

Instead of launching a crash programme to rebuild houses, hostels and hotels, which would have benefited the shell-shocked inhabitants by creating jobs and pumping cash into a derelict economy, the newly arrived UN lavished millions on the Olympia, a bobbing tribute to expatriate comfort and an object of disgust to locals.

The Hotel Olympia was the UN Transitional Administration in East Timor's (UNTAET) first public relations blunder. The second was the attempt to build a new national authority, dominated by international civil servants, with no East Timorese in senior positions. Though a National Consultative Committee (NCC) was created, incorporating elements of the National Council for East Timorese Resistance (CNRT), as an advisory body, UNTAET's first six months in office

2000, Dili in ruins – Credit: Tom Fawthrop

largely continued the island's tradition of government by foreigners, ruling benevolently in this case, but no less arbitrarily.

UNTAET's chief executive, Sergio Vieira de Mello, admitted in March that the interim government lacked credibility and that a process of 'Timorisation' must begin soon. Apologists pointed out that the UN had never before been called upon to function in a 'Year Zero' environment of total infrastructural and institutional meltdown. It had to determine what currency (rupiah, escudo or Australian dollar) to use and, more controversially, what should be the new nation's official language. Lisbon had made the adoption of Portuguese the condition of its meeting the cost of government for the next five years – though only 20% of the population still speak it. Little wonder it began to dawn on the East Timorese that what they were witnessing was a wave of recolonisation by the international community.

In the same month, Professor Jarat Chopra, veteran of 12 UN missions, resigned from his UNTAET post in protest at what he depicted as 'UN Czars who carve out bureaucratic fiefdoms, without any genuine concern for the mission and the people of East Timor'. In an article for the *Journal of the International Institute for Strategic Studies*, he wrote: 'Integral to repeated failures of [UN] peace missions is a hierarchical system that cannot adapt to the novel mandates and the unique conditions of each deployment.' By way of confirming UNTAET's perceived extravagance, Vieira de Mello recently revealed that of the funds so far allocated as aid or grants to East Timor, US$680 million had been spent on UN peacekeeping, policing and relief operations, and only US$59 million was allocated for reconstruction. The most visible fruits of independence appeared to be falling at the feet of the UN's legion of foreign private contractors.

However, UNTAET's performance in the field receives unusual praise. A July report, by the independent – and frequently critical – East Timor Institute for Reconstruction and Monitoring (ETIRM), which brings together UN agencies and 60 Timorese NGOs, called the UN's humanitarian relief effort 'highly successful' and praised the aid agencies' 'coordination, commitment and flexibility'. The timely delivery of relief supplies had prevented any major food emergencies, while basic public services – electricity, water supply and health – were back up and running. Immigration, customs, taxation and a postal system have all reportedly been re-established and donors have funded the launch of two newspapers, the *Timor Post* and the Timorese-language *Lalenok* (*Index 2/2000*), and three radio stations.

One of the ETIRM's most significant criticisms was the lack of communication between the UN and international agencies on the one hand, and the East Timorese on the other. 'Certainly the chaotic nature of the situation in East Timor in the aftermath of September's violence made effective international – East Timorese collaboration difficult … At the same time, it would seem that the UN and many international NGOs did not make effective East Timorese participation a priority.'

By April, this sense of exclusion had evolved into a daily demonstration by Timorese outside UNTAET's Dili headquarters. In June, José 'Xanana' Gusmao, the former resistance leader now released from his Jakarta imprisonment and the man most likely to become East Timor's first elected president, threatened to boycott an international donors conference in Lisbon unless UNTAET displayed greater transparency over funding and devolved more power locally. Vieira de Mello announced that four of the eight interim government ministries were to be handed over to Timorese, and that the size of the NCC would be doubled. Gusmao went to Lisbon.

Mari Alkatiri, the new minister of economic affairs in the transitional government, has the daunting task of making East Timor pay its own way, something that neither Indonesia nor Portugal ever managed in over 400 years of coffee-growing and timber-felling. The best hope is that Dili can tap revenue from the proven oil and gas reserves in the Timor Gap, which Australian companies are planning to bring ashore in Darwin. Yet the prospect of great oil wealth – one intimately allied with the dream of independence from Indonesia – may yet turn out to be a dream postponed. As an Australian official in Dili told the *Australian* recently: 'UNTAET knows it can only establish the basic services. This is going to be a very poor country for a very long time, and we cannot build what the East Timorese cannot then afford to run.'

Hand in glove with the search for economic viability are public calls for justice for the mayhem orchestrated by the Indonesian military in September last year. At the peak of Operation Clean Sweep, the US suspended military ties with Jakarta and the World Bank froze its aid. By November, the US Congress had made the resumption of aid conditional on effective prosecution of the military and militia members responsible for human rights atrocities in East Timor, and the return of some 120,000 East Timorese held against their will over the border in Indonesian West Timor. On 31 January 2000, an international commission of inquiry concluded that the systematic and large-scale nature of the crimes in East Timor warranted the establishment of an international tribunal. President Abdurrahman Wahid then argued that Indonesia be allowed to take responsibility for prosecuting human rights violators itself. In deference to the fragility of Jakarta's new democracy, the international tribunal was temporarily shelved. By July this year, the US military were conducted joint exercises with Indonesian troops. The prospect of any kind of trial is receding: justice is hostage to the upheavals inside the archipelago and in East Timor itself. Military-backed militias have been stepping up their cross-border raids in recent months, killing two UN peacekeepers and several East Timorese.

Paramilitary pressure on East Timor's western border could trigger a backlash from Fretilin, the 5,000-strong former guerrilla army that has been dormant under UN supervision. On 4 September, Xanana Gusmao told *Newsweek* that, to counter the militia threat, 'we should strike back and destroy them inside West Timor'. The comment drew an immediate ripost from Indonesia's military high command: 'search-and-destroy missions' would risk embroiling UN forces in open battle with a fellow UN member, dragging out the UNTAET presence for years. But with Australia and New Zealand both seeking exit strategies, the threat of cross-border incursions could evolve into a bargaining chip.

An emboldened Jakarta has since begun to honour its obligations to the UN in the letter only. On 18 August, the People's Assembly approved an amendment to the constitution granting immunity to former president Suharto on corruption charges, and the Indonesian armed forces for crimes against humanity. Armed with this clause, the attorney-general's office announced on 1 September that it would question 19 provisional suspects in its investigation into the violence in East Timor; absent from the list was the name of General Wiranto, the army chief in East Timor widely credited with organising the pro-Indonesian militias in the first place. Such blatant disregard could prompt the UN to step up its calls for the formation of an international tribune but, one year on, time could be on the Indonesians' side. ❏

Tom Fawthrop *is a freelance journalist based in South East Asia. He was one of the last reporters to leave Dili during the Indonesian onslaught last September*

JOHN WADHAM

Rights now

The director of human rights pressure group Liberty examines the implementation of Britain's new Human Rights Act, and the likely clashes with recently passed controversial legislation

The Human Rights Act will come into force on 2 October. It incorporates the European Convention on Human Rights into domestic law and is the most significant human rights reform for many years. For the first time, rights such as privacy and family life, freedom of expression and assembly, the right to a fair trial, freedom from arbitrary arrest, and freedom from discrimination will be enshrined in domestic law. Those who claim that their rights have been breached will no longer necessarily have to go to the European Court of Human Rights in Strasbourg.

The act will not be a panacea. The Convention's age is clearly discernible from the weakness of its equality provisions, and it is silent on important issues such as the rights of children and standards in prisons. The limitations it places on rights are too broad, and the anti-discrimination provisions too narrow. The act will apply to all public authorities performing a public function. It does not impose duties on private individuals or companies unless they are performing public functions.

Public authorities have now had two years since the act passed in 1998 to change their policies and procedures, so most of what they do will comply. However, there will be a considerable number of unintentional violations, public authorities will make mistakes and in some cases will have good reasons for not wanting to go quite as far in changing as they should. Where there has been a breach of the Convention (or even where there is about to be) the victim can take proceedings in court. They may be able to obtain an injunction to stop the violation, force the public authority to take action, or obtain damages and compensation.

The Human Rights Act will mean a new interpretation of old (and new) laws. Old judge-made law (the common law) will have to change if it does not respect the Convention. Nearly all secondary legislation (like Statutory Instruments) will not be valid if it doesn't comply. Even primary legislation (Parliamentary statute) 'so far as it is possible to do so' will have to be brought into line with Convention rights. However, if primary legislation cannot be read to comply with the Convention, the higher courts can make what is called a 'declaration of incompatibility', which will allow the government to amend that law speedily.

All this looks very good, but how will the act mesh with other legislation that has emerged from Parliament over the last session? The first thing to notice is section 19 of the act, which imposes a duty on ministers who are introducing new bills to make a 'statement of compatibility'. Unfortunately, the government's approach to section 19 statements has significantly reduced its usefulness. In assessing whether a particular provision complies, those advising the government assume that all those public authorities that have to implement the provision will act in compliance with the Convention if they have the power to do so.

To see how this works it is worth looking at a measure like the Terrorism Act 2000. In what Liberty sees as one of many unacceptable provisions, the act made it a criminal offence for a person to encourage support for a proscribed organisation by merely speaking at a meeting. The maximum sentence for this offence is six months' jail.

It also makes it an offence to speak at the same meeting as someone speaking for a proscribed organisation. This would have had the peculiar result of those who wanted to oppose an organisation being guilty of an offence if they spoke out.

The government was happy to say this complied with the act – the argument being that to give discretion to the police to act in ways which would clearly violate the Convention can still be assessed as 'Convention compliant', because the discretion exercised by the police would be constrained by the provisions of the Human Rights Act.

The Regulation of Investigatory Powers Act is due to come into force in October. This measure was created primarily to legalise the previously unregulated conduct of the police and other law enforcement agencies when using covert and intrusive surveillance. Until that act comes into force those agencies will be in violation of Article 8, the right to privacy, because their surveillance activities were not 'in accordance with the law'.

Unfortunately, the government used the opportunity to extend the powers of the police and others. Equally problematic is the lack of safeguards in the act. For instance the act allows the home secretary to authorise telephones taps; in some circumstances the police themselves can authorise the use of bugging devices and the police will need no independent authorisation before they can obtain the details of every phone call you have made. In Liberty's view there should be a requirement that all surveillance should be authorised by a court.

The Football (Disorder) Bill gives powers to the police to prevent people travelling to international football matches without needing to prove that the person concerned has been convicted of a criminal offence. This bill may violate the Convention, but the failure of the government to incorporate into the Human Rights Act the rights of freedom of movement in Protocol 4 to the European Convention means that any challenges will arise because of the free movement provision from the law of the European Union and not the Human Rights Act.

The Human Rights Act will lead to challenges of new and exisiting law. Also, given that Parliament failed to restrict legislation to what is allowable under the Human Rights Act, the necessary restrictions will have to be imposed by, say, the police on themselves instead. Inevitably this will lead to more challenges. Liberty is planning some of these challenges and I am confident that the Human Rights Act will certainly be the most important extension in our own 70-year history and possibly since the Bill of Rights in 1688. ❏

John Wadham is a solicitor and director of Liberty. More at www.liberty-human-rights.org.uk

BRAM POSTHUMUS

The mask slips

London, the libel honeypot, is about to lure another alleged human rights violator – President Charles Taylor of Liberia

No court date has yet been set for a trial that will pit Liberia's President Charles Taylor against Stephen Ellis, a research associate at the University of Leiden Africa Studies Centre and author of *Mask of Anarchy* (Hurst & Co, London), a widely acclaimed book on Liberia's civil war. In January this year, Taylor instituted libel proceedings against Ellis, his publisher and *The Times* of London over passages in the book that portray him eating the flesh and drinking the blood of his enemies. The offending excerpts are quotes from Taylor's own former defence minister, Tom Woewiyu, now a senator in Monrovia after winning a by-election in the Bassa constituency.

Ellis and his lawyer mounted a detailed defence, which they filed in June. 'It's not just a document, it's more like a whole dossier,' says Ellis, who is confident he will win. 'Everything we say we can justify.' Ellis is adamant that all the information that found its way into *Mask of Anarchy* can stand up to close scrutiny. Taylor's lawyers have not so far responded, but all indications are that Taylor will persist with his legal battle.

The specific allegations that have upset Taylor are mentioned twice in the book amid a catalogue of other horrors, mostly against civilians, committed by factions on all sides. Compared to some of these, Taylor's own National Patriotic Front of Liberia receives relatively good notices. No one is spared, including the Nigerian-led peacekeeping group ECOMOG, which Ellis alleges took part in looting, corruption and drug-dealing. 'I've heard it said that some of those close to Taylor have actually read the book and say they like it because it's balanced,' says Ellis. What's not clear is whether the Liberian president has read it.

Given these apparently favourable comments and the fact that Woewiyu, author of the allegations of cannibalism, is still in Monrovia, the question arises why the trial is taking place at all. Apart from the personal element – Taylor's ego is said to be easily stung – there are two theories. The first, and most plausible, is Liberia's historic obsession with image. The government is working overtime to convince the world that it possesses a functioning administration that could work as a stabilising factor in the West African region. The capture by rebels in May of some 500 UN peacekeepers in neighbouring Sierra Leone was something of a godsend. Here was Taylor in a favourite role, the honest broker, a task made easier by the fact that the hostages were held by his friend and ally Foday Sankoh. Whoever detracts from that carefully crafted image, journalists or opposition politicians, is quickly declared an enemy of the state.

The *New Democrat*, one of the few Liberian newspapers not owned by Taylor's media empire, suspended operations in mid-July and its staff went into hiding after persistent government harassment. The threats became especially virulent after the death, in July, of Vice-President Enoch Dogolea amid widespread speculation on the cause of his passing. *New Democrat* was specifically warned by Taylor that he would now become 'ferocious'. In August, former presidential candidate Ellen Johnson-Sirleaf called for Taylor to be arraigned before a tribunal that the UN is setting up to try war crimes in Sierra Leone, in particular, those committed by Foday Sankoh's Revolutionary United Front. Three weeks later, her name appeared on a list of 15 exiled Liberians who were to be charged with treason in connection with the activities of a new Liberian rebel group in Lofa County, bordering Guinea and Sierra Leone.

The government is particularly sensitive about foreign reporters. On 21 August, a four-member TV crew filming for Britain's Channel 4, was arrested and accused of filming in no-go areas, seeking to damage the country's image and spying. The crew, led by the award-winning Sierra Leonean film-maker Sorious Samura, was held in jail in Monrovia for five days, although the government was fully aware of its activities and had officially accredited them as journalists. Nelson Mandela, Manchester City's Liberian football star George Weah and one of Taylor's few US friends, Jesse Jackson, all pleaded on the journalists' behalf before the charges were dropped and the crew allowed to go. Most illuminating was a subsequent statement by the Liberian ambassador in South Africa who, without offering any apology, lamented that the whole episode was bad for Liberia's image abroad.

The second theory behind the London trial revolves around the anxieties of supporters abroad, who rely upon Taylor's largesse for their own survival. The source of his patronage, Sierra Leone's diamond fields, is now less secure than at any time in recent years: at home, the UN is considering operations to remove the diamond fields from rebel hands; abroad moves are under way to ban the trade in 'conflict diamonds'. The revenue to be won from a successful libel case, runs the theory, would go some way towards keeping Taylor's foreign-based support intact.

Far from clearing his name, the trial is likely to prove another shot in Taylor's foot. His government faces international sanctions over diamond smuggling and gun-running while, in Liberia, he relies on paramilitary armies to consolidate control of the population. To win the case, he will have to come to London to testify. If he does, the result – Pinochet-style – is likely to be the kind of tribunal he has always resisted at home. 'He never wanted a Truth and Reconciliation Commission or a War Crimes Tribunal,' remarked one observer in Monrovia. 'Now that he is going ahead with the trial, we will finally have one anyway. Let him go and testify. I would be delighted to see him defend himself during cross-examination.' ❏

Bram Posthumus, *a freelance journalist based in the Netherlands, is a specialist on West Africa*

VERAN MATIC

All out for change

'Nobody's candle burns till dawn', goes the Serb adage wistfully. So is this month's presidential election a sunrise or the glow of new-lit fires?

Today is 18 August. There are 35 days to go before elections on 24 September. Polling is scheduled at the federal level (Serbia and Montenegro), the local and provincial level (in Serbia and Vojvodina) and there will be elections for the presidency of the Former Republic of Yugoslavia (FRY). This would be reason enough for intense anxiety even in a country more democratic than FRY today: it opens up the increasingly problematic relationship between Serbia and Montenegro; President Slobodan Milosevic's decision to stand for a further term is potentially hazardous; and the expression of anything remotely critical is vigorously repressed.

Where does that leave the media and election coverage? Yugoslavia's largest independent weekly *Vreme* has chosen the 'US' way. In a recent editorial, the magazine openly supported the presidential nomination of opposition candidate Vojislav Kostunica, leader of the Democratic Party of Serbia, the man around whom the formerly fragmented and squabbbling opposition parties have united. For local and regional radio stations, dependent on relations with local authorities, this is not an option.

All serious research shows that the greatest danger in the elections is low voter turnout. If it is less that 70%, the disciplined mass of pro-regime voters, estimated at around 25% of the total electorate, could easily hand victory to Milosevic in the first round of the election, particularly now that the constitution has been changed to abolish the 50% minimum turnout. This also makes opposition boycott of the elections ineffective.

Traditionally, the young, for the majority anti-regime, have been the biggest group of abstainers, convinced that the nature of the opposition made any change impossible as long as Milosevic was alive. Today, things are different: the opposition is seemingly together and Milosevic can be defeated. Discontent is widespread – about 75% of Serbs say they want 'thorough change'. The independent media, particularly radio and TV, have made voter turnout a key issue, encouraging people to vote without necessarily prescribing a choice.

The reaction has been fierce. The regime has prepared for a confrontation with civil society and the media with far greater thoroughness than with the democratic opposition (*Index* 3/2000). The Public Information Act and the University Act, adopted in 1998, were the prelude both to the war in Kosovo and the final showdown with the pro-democracy forces in Serbia and Montenegro. The indictment of Milosevic and his closest associates by The Hague Tribunal further accelerated the pace, with senior members of the government accusing the independent media and members of Otpor – the student-based opposition grouping – of treason and terrorism.

Last May, Radio B2-92 was evicted for the second time and banned for the fourth when police took over the only privately owned city television station, Studio B, claiming that the broadcaster had called for violence and rebellion against the authorities. Using satellite and the Internet, Radio B2-92 news programmes were re-established within a few hours and are now rebroadcast by local radio. In towns with no local media, people download news from the website and distribute it by hand. TV and radio programmes made by ANEM, Radio B2-92 and other independents are also rebroadcast by other media in south-east Europe, many of which are can be picked up back in FRY. In this way a network of stations has been established in the area covered by the OSCE's Pact for Stability in South-East Europe. The media throughout the region share the same difficulties: the lack of democratisation in the region. By linking stations and exchanging programmes, a new form of resistance to censorship has emerged as a result of government repression.

Public surveys show a massive drop in the prevalence of nationalist and populist ideas. Two years ago, 40% of Serbs said they wanted to live in an ethnically homogenous country, now that has dropped to 12%, close to the European average for xenophobia. That rate of change owes more to the independent media, NGOs and especially the mass movement Otpor, a popular rebuff to Serbia's old-style opposition leaders, than to the international community. The latter is more interested in the occasional arrest of suspected war criminals than the domestic process of truth and reconciliation. For instance, when General Radislav Krstic speaks at The Hague about the killing of Muslims in Srebrenica in July 1995 (*Index* 2/1998), the independent media now report the testimony verbatim.

Milosevic is discredited and has lost all legitimacy. If the electorate force him to compete in a second round by not giving him an absolute majority in the first, the end of his era is in sight. But the end of Milosevic is only the beginning of a much bigger task: the modernisation and democratisation of the country and stabilisation of the region generally. ❏

Veran Matic is co-founder and editor-in-chief of Radio B92 Belgrade and chairman of the Association of Independent Electronic Media (ANEM)

MARY KENNY

Women as censors

Censorship by women has a long and, in most cases, honourable history

Recently, a colleague of mine – an executive on a London newspaper – received a pornographic picture through her email system. It was from a male writer she employed from time to time. She was appalled. She wasn't 'shocked' in the Victorian-spinster sense; she was disgusted by the man's lack of judgment and she felt a wave of personal revulsion. She disliked having her working space thus invaded.

I too receive scores of emails each week which offer me pornographic packages, because my email address has appeared in the public realm. They are a confounded vexation, and I resent having to pay to receive such drivel. If you delete one sender, another soon takes its place, offering 'hot and horny' images of 'young teens' and 'great fucks' with 'hot Asian babes'. However, I wearily accept that the price of freedom of communication means being sent a lot of lowering material by nerds and assholes and I rise above it as best I can.

Women, in the majority, have never much liked pornography and have, historically, been in the forefront of campaigns to censor or control sexually explicit or violent material. There are some women who do not object to pornography; there are some women who may enjoy it; there are women who work in the pornography or sex industry and claim to do so voluntarily. There are female libertarians who hold that liberty means also accepting the dross and the squalid. But when all is said and done, women have always been active in objecting to the free circulation of sexually explicit words and images, and have been most vocal in finding such material offensive.

From the uncompromising feminist academics such as Catharine MacKinnon, whose influential book *Only Words* argues that words themselves are the very agency of inequality, racial and sexual harassment, and sexual offences against women and children, to the doughty old Christian campaigner, Mary Whitehouse, who tried to keep explicit sex off the TV screens in Britain, women of left and right have proved themselves sisters under the skin in calling for, and upholding, forms of censorship. I realised that this alliance was seamless when I was speaking at a debate on sex in the media at Cambridge University about 15 years ago. Mary Whitehouse was on her feet excoriating the porn merchants who were exploiting and degrading our civilisation; and in the audience she was being heartily cheered by a group of boiler-suited lesbians with clenched fists: 'Right on, Mary!' She took it in good heart, and afterwards there was much sisterly hugging all round. The combination of Christian right and lesbian left won the debate, by the way.

Germaine Greer has said, on several occasions, that the sex revolution and the feminist revolution have been erroneously conflated. They are considered to be of the same order, and in some areas of culture there is common ground. A magazine such as *Cosmopolitan* – the market leader – unblushingly promotes more orgasms and the freedom to have 'great sex', and at the same time takes a feminist position on women's rights: here the two 'revolutions' of sex and feminism do appear to merge. (Clive James, Greer's fellow Australian, once famously described 'women's liberation' as 'more pussy on the market', and the *Cosmo* message bears out his aphorism.)

But historically there were marked differences between the sex revolution and the women's revolution, and these tensions will, in my view, always reappear. I am a biological determinist in that I believe men and women to be by nature different; that 'custom will never conquer Nature', as Cicero said, and that attitudes to freedom and responsibility are, by biological mandate, contrasting in men and women. Women will never, in the majority, feel as easy about freedom of sexual expression as men, in the majority, do: those emails and electronic images are, *ipso facto*, images and texts about young girls offered as a commercial service, and the instinctive female interpretation of such material is quite often a feeling of humiliation. That is the way it is, and will remain. There will not be 'equality' whereby men's bodies are offered to women, because females are not sexually aroused by visualising the male merely as an anatomy.

The feminist movement of the nineteenth century arose from a variety of roots – educational, political, literary. But feminism always had a distinctive religious strand. Englishwomen as social campaigners were usually formed in a religious faith: Elizabeth Fry, Florence Nightingale, Josephine Butler. And in the United States itself, feminism was born out of the anti-slavery movement in which Protestant evangelical women were so active.

Early feminism was about emancipating women to be educated, to be political, to own property and acquire more entitlements over their own lives; but it was also, to some extent, about controlling the power, and the sexuality, of men. Christabel Pankhurst's celebrated slogan 'Votes for Women, and Chastity for Men' said it all. Women were to be politically empowered; and men were to be restrained from their lascivious practices, which included using brothels and spreading venereal disease to innocent women (such as King Edward VII who gave his inoffensive queen, Alexandra, the venereal disease that he had picked up on his Continental canoodlings).

There were feminists who were sexual liberals: but such feminists – Christabel's sister Sylvia, for instance – were usually also politically committed elsewhere (they were often communists or socialists). The sexual radicals, such as Havelock Ellis, George Bernard Shaw and then the Bloomsbury group, also included women, but all in all, the sex revolution was more of a 'man's movement'. Marie Stopes received many more letters from men than from women – partly because men were financially responsible for begetting children at this period, but also because men welcomed sexual freedom. In the culture wars which followed the rise to celebrity of Marie Stopes, it is possible that as many women were opposed to Stopes as were for her.

Cate Haste's study, *Rules of Desire: Sex in Britain, from World War I*, published in 1992, chronicles the extraordinary rise in sexually puritanical women vigilantes, after WWI, patrolling the parks for courting couples, monitoring the cinemas for scandalous sex scenes, and disapproving of the 'dirty books' that were becoming available through mass distribution. The ringleaders of these women censors were quite often ex-suffragettes. A most colourful example was Damer Dawson, a wealthy feminist philanthropist, Alpine mountainer and pioneering motorist: she was the guiding light of the Women's Police Volunteers patrolling parks and towpaths in London to ensure that young girls were not behaving foolishly (ie sexually). She was also obsessed with rescuing women from 'the white slave traffic', and, more realisticially, with assisting Belgian refugees made homeless by wartime.

Damer Dawson's associates included Mary Allen, a window-smashing suffragette, and Nina Boyle, whose concern was unfair treatment of women under the law. These feminists fought for women's rights: and they deplored the sexual licence which they saw as part of women's exploitation. Throughout the 1920s and 30s, sexual liberals were pitched against purity leaguers resisting the onward march of more openly explicit books and movies. These purity leagues were certainly backed by the Churches: but they were also most emphatically backed by women. In the US, the prohibition introduced in 1919 was overwhelmingly a 'woman's movement', according to Andrew Sinclair's history of prohibition: a different form of social control – the censorship of alcohol.

In Irish social history, which is my particular area of interest, the rise of literary censorship – which was brought in by law in 1929, and relaxed, or liberalised, in 1967 – is often associated with the dominance of the Catholic Church in the early years of the Irish state. The Irish state did reflect the values of Irish Catholicism; but it is also clear that women played an important role in supporting the Church's values and in instigating and upholding censorship. In the early period of the Celtic Renaissance, Maud Gonne – who was, of course, WB Yeats's muse, and an iconic national figure – founded a feminist organistion called *Inghinidhe na hEirean* (Daughters of Ireland), which is frequently cited as a source of Irishwomen's empowerment. It did some good educational work, but its agenda was also cultural and sexual censorship: its mission statement included the aim to 'discourage the reading and circulation of low English literature, the attending of vulgar English entertainments at the theatres and music halls, and to combat in every way English influence, which is doing so much injury to the artistic taste and refinement of the Irish people'. Upon this agenda, the mentality for the Irish censorship was constructed and, by around 1911, reports of the 'Ladies Vigilante Committees' were beginning to appear in the religious press. These ladies' groups would monitor the theatres, the new medium of the cinema, and books.

The Irish Censorship Board, set up after legislation in 1929, was not so much a cowled inquisition of priests as a democratically responsive body: it invited members of the public to submit books considered deleterious to public morals. We do not know who submitted the many candidates for censorship, but it is very likely that women played a leading role. In his study of Irish literary censorship – regarded as the standard text – the academic Michael Adams notes that local library committees, often headed by a woman librarian, were influential in submitting books to be banned. (Then, as now, women read more fiction than men.) In memoirs and autobiographies, such as Sean O'Faoilain's and the poet Austin Clarke's, the greater book-burners were their mothers.

The religious press in Ireland had a strong feminine participation, as can be seen from subscription lists, letters and requests for prayers, and there were frequent calls for more, not less, censorship. This also appeared in the secular press.

Women feel more threatened by sexually explicit material and, as mothers, I think women also have an impulse to protect the young from what they see as brutal or squalid. Women also have an urge to control the depredations of men, who are, biologically, still the more promiscuous sex.

Younger women today are, it may be argued, less prudish than women used to be – the success of *Cosmo* and its imitators demonstrates that. With more freedom, more access to opportunity and equality, and with the fear of sex reduced by birth control, it may be that women don't need to retreat into the 'refinements' of traditional femininity. It may be that the feminine, and feminist, urge to prohibit may be modifying. But biological psychology does not change profoundly, in my view, and censorship and control arise in many new ways. Political Correctness – the exasperatingly genteel cloak of euphemism falling over so many sexual and racial facts of life – is one of them. But that, as they say, is another story. ❏

Mary Kenny's *social history of Ireland in the twentieth century*, Goodbye to Catholic Ireland *is published in paperback by New Island Books, Dublin, in September 2000*

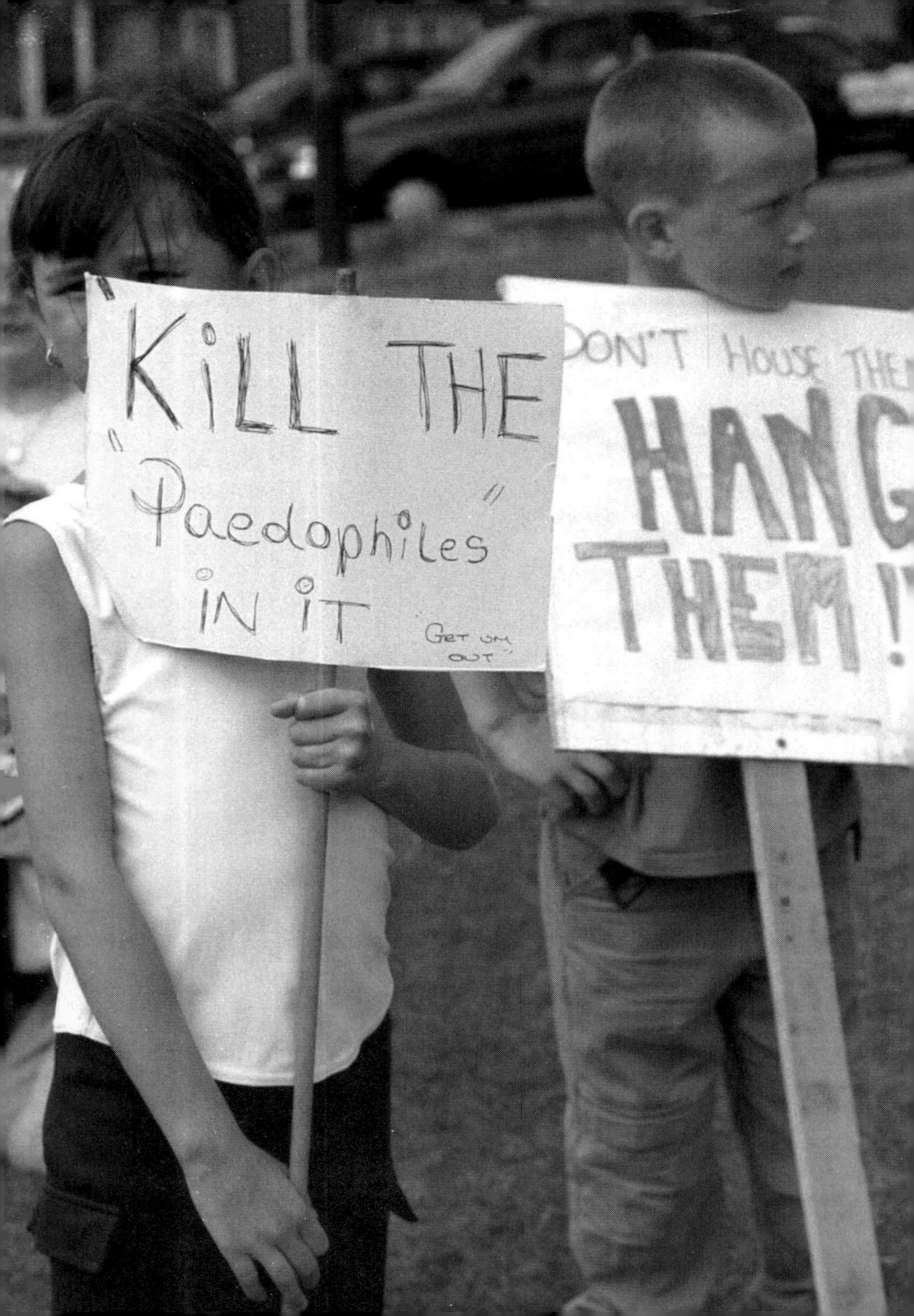
"KiLL THE "Paedophiles" IN iT
GET UM OUT"
DON'T HOUSE
HANG THEM!

Manufacturing monsters

And all the little monsters said in a chorus:
You must kiss us.

What! You who are evil,
Ugly and uncivil.
You who are cruel...

Yes, you must bless us.

But the evil you do,
The endless ado.
Why bless you?...

Because, said the monsters, beginning to laugh,
You might as well. You are part of us ❏

Suniti Namjoshi

Guest editor, Julian Petley

STANLEY COHEN

Some thoroughly modern monsters

The failed July 2000 round of the US-staged Israeli-Palestinian 'peace process' in Camp David opened with an unstaged photo-opportunity for the world's media. Chairman Arafat and Prime Minister Barak, watched by a beaming President Clinton, graciously jostle each other to be first to enter the room. The CNN subtext could have been printed: 'Two leaders, so long deep enemies, their sides locked in murderous conflict for generations – look, they are ordinary people after all.' With just a little mediation by the benign superpower – Clinton is urging them *both* through the door – they have become human.

Needless to say, this is not how everyone, especially those living inside this conflict, saw things. To some Israeli Jews, Yasser Arafat remains the same monster 'inside' but has changed his social identity into someone human enough to do business with, even live beside. Many others will never concede even this limited transformation; and for them, Ehud Barak, the military hero, is now a traitor, his arms literally around the monster's shoulder. For many Palestinians, Barak is yet another duplicitous Zionist leader and Arafat a servile old clown, getting ready for another sell-out. Neither side takes too seriously the notion of a US president as an even-handed 'mediator'.

Moral passages are always partial and fragile. Compare Arafat's slow progress with the somewhat fuller demonsterisation of Gerry Adams and the near total success of Nelson Mandela (never a monster internationally but his moral authority and aura finally accepted even by white South Africans). Media clichés about reconciliation and humanisation invariably run counter to traditional beliefs that monsters only fake their rehabilitation and will inevitably revert to true character. Thus, former colonial terrorists claim 'freedom fighter' status, become more-or-less democratic leaders then, after a political crisis, return to being monsters. Robert Mugabe conveniently follows this script.

Mundane monsters are becoming easier to make. In an age of 'in-depth' profiles, investigative journalism and intrusive biography, public figures of unblemished or even saintly status can be vilified instantly. It appears that 'all along' or 'under the surface' they were ruthless and cruel, dishonest or sexually depraved. Who believes all this? Well, it turns out that just about everybody does.

Some grand political monsters (and their apologists) try hard to erase their moral blemishes. 'You can't blame me,' they say, borrowing from the cultural scripts of excuses and sad tales routinely used by their underlings. 'They didn't tell me anything ... I had no choice ... I was just following orders ... these were isolated incidents.' 'It was more complicated than you think' is a more sophisticated tale: neither apology (I was wrong, forgive me) nor justification (I was right, exonerate me) but the radical demand to understand that 'things were different then' and, therefore, that 'if you had been there you would have done the same'. In some political circumstances – notably when so many were active collaborators or passive colluders – these tales are credited. More often, they are dismissed as patently bogus and self-serving: alibis designed to obtain a pardon or amnesty. The hardest tale to fake is 'seeing the light'. This is to acknowledge that you were wrong all the time: the secular version of confession, conversion, expiation, remorse, or their therapeutic equivalent, 'self-insight.'

Other public monsters, of course, do not seek benign relabelling – neither by a Nuremberg trial nor a truth commission. After the Fall, they still refuse to accept that what they did was wrong at the time. Thus Stalin, Mao, Hitler and Pol Pot or, more recently, Idi Amin, Mobutu, Ceausescu, the Argentinian generals, the Burmese SLORC. History will show that they were saviours, not monsters. In the chilling words of Admiral Emilio Massera, the convicted member of the Argentine junta: 'I am responsible but not guilty. My judges may have the chronicle, but History belongs to me and that is where the final verdict will be decided.' This continued self-righteousness ensures that no amount of historical revisionism ('Pol Pot: The Family Man Behind the Headlines') can cleanse their monstrosity. General Pinochet's moral blemishes endured Lady Thatcher praising him as a saviour who had 'restored' democracy to Chile.

'In the animal kingdom,' wrote Thomas Szasz, ' the rule is eat or be eaten; in the human kingdom, define or be defined.' Thus, taking over the television station is so emblematic of modern political revolutions. (And this is why issues of censorship and freedom of speech are important: Gerry Adams was kept off British television not because of the unlikely prospect that he would convert anyone to the IRA cause, but because there was a possibility that he would seem more human.) The release of political prisoners is an even more resonant emblem of political change. First, all sides must agree on who the 'political prisoners' are: the ANC list was obviously longer than the apartheid government's. (A unique commission in Namibia actually set up guidelines for determining the political status of prisoners.) After the final round of epistemological politics is negotiated, yesterday's monsters walk out of their cages, in a scripted public ceremony. The release of the last batch of Republican prisoners from the Maze prison was extraordinary – not because of protest from Loyalists or disgust from victims, but because of the ease with which bombers and mass killers (such as Sean Kelly who killed nine people in the Shankill Road massacre) emerged into the light. The Good Friday agreement decreed that 428 political prisoners be released – and look, there they go, to the acclaim of their families and old comrades, and more like the prisoners of war they always claimed to be than the terrorists they were. The mother who reminds us that 'he killed my son' is almost offstage, an embarrassing voice from the past.

If the unrecalcitrant ideologues back on the streets are from the other side, this proves that they really always were fanatics; if they are from our side, we praise their faith during the dark years, but mumble our disavowal of their methods. Repentance is no easy matter. Critics of the South African Truth and Reconciliation Commission are deeply uncomfortable about giving immunity to offenders who publicly express a remorse that cannot be 'genuine'. So many people proclaim that 'inwardly' they were always against apartheid, it appears that *no one ever* supported the system. These liars have to be exposed and shamed, their bad faith carefully dissected in public. Victims suffer when they see minor monsters quietly slip back into the new moral order and major monsters ceremonially released. But perhaps they need not burden themselves further by worrying whether their tormentors' contrition is sincere, whether they really feel remorse or what inner voices haunt them. To preserve today's promise of democracy and social justice, the old bastards should tell the truth – and then be swept away by history. As long as they promise to behave themselves, why require them to be sincere or sensitive?

It is more productive to redefine and exonerate the victims. Ritual arrangements can cleanse their identity and reputation: police files searched to find the falsely accused, the arbitrarily arrested and the tortured. 'Freeze-dried' stigmas can be unfrozen as a gesture of reparation to living victims and the families and friends of the dead. This politics of vindication requires two acknowledgements from the old regime. First, to admit that apartheid (or its equivalent elsewhere) was not just a 'mistake', 'irrelevant', 'coming to a dead end', a 'closed book'; nor what ex-president de Klerk referred to (as late as March 1992) as something that 'started in idealism in the quest for justice'. These are wholly inadequate acknowledgements of the deliberate suffering caused. Second, to concede that the opposition's cause was justified: that is, people were victimised not because they were wrong or bad, but because they were right and good.

Reconciliation is impossible without full knowledge of what you are being reconciled to. 'Learning to live with each other' does not mean 'Drawing a line on the past', still less 'No one has clean hands.' Perpetrators who pardon themselves and asssume the right to be magnanimous by closing the book on the past hardly deserve a sympathetic relabelling.

In all societies, the past is continuously adapted and revised to reflect shifts in current ideology and political agenda. The communist style was overt: people are, in Kundera's memorable phrase, 'airbrushed' out of history, too monstrous even to be looked at. They can be restored later, no longer monsters, when previously unacceptable ideas become widespread. Upheaval is followed by purges, then by rewriting history.

This making and unmaking of political monsters is a calculated strategy in totalitarian societies; it occurs naturally in traditional societies but is also used selectively in modern democracies. In post-modern mass culture and media, however, this is less a moral passage than an identity passage. In Disneyland 'history', the past is not deliberately obliterated and rewritten in the Orwellian sense but evaporates in the cacophony of the present. In a media regime of personal profiles, instant character assassination, quasi-information and docusoaps that purport to be true, the past is erased without need for censorship, propaganda and a Ministry of Truth – nor a meta-theory of what is right and wrong. This cultural amnesia allows the monsters and victims of atrocities in distant places (East Timor, Paraguay, Rwanda, Cambodia, Ethiopia, Guatemala) to slip into a premature pre-history. These victims were never important enough for us to consider their tormentors.

Alongside this type of forgetting, western democratic societies still encourage the more traditional rewriting of history. The astonishing shifts in US foreign policy are less post-modern than textbook Orwellian: last year's ally and favoured arms customer (whether Saddam, Mobutu or Noriega) becomes today's enemy; today's 'emerging democracy' was last year's terrorist state. As Chomsky points out, the US government does not even attempt any principled justification; a total transformation is merely a 'change of course'.

In the mass media and popular culture of 'normal' societies, the iconography of monsters seems more contingent on fashion than ideology. Lady Diana changes from the nation's 'princess of hearts' to the psycho-pathological monster (narcissistic, calculating, bulimic and 'in denial') then moves all the way back for deification. Celebrities are allowed, even required to change: they just keep on being 'outed' or 'coming out'.

There are, however, only a fixed and limited number of slots for non-political deviants to become public monsters. The term 'folk devils' that I used 30 years ago to describe the media construction of the mods and rockers is more benign. It remains adequate for the cultural updates of skinheads, punks, hippies and social drug users. The moral panic line is crossed when the problem is seen as too horrible and its risk too threatening for mere cultural boundary-setting. For this, we need *true victims*: their suffering is obvious and they are unambiguously victims (totally helpless and with no hint of 'bringing it on themselves'). We also need *essentialist offenders*: their actions are not the product of fashion, situation, setting, opportunity or chance, but express the essence of the type of person they are and always will be.

The recent waves of football hooliganism nearly reached these bench-marks. For 30 years, British football hooligans were merely cast from the same old working-class yobbos: lumpen louts stimulated by too much alcohol and media attention. They were always, of course, different from the *real* fans and supporters. More recently, though, this difference became seen as a fixed psychological essence and moral character. Louts, proposed Prime Minister Tony Blair, could be stopped by the police for being, well, 'louts'. Further, their essence would be literally captured – by a list of names and photos. Whatever you had done (or been suspected of doing), whether you were convicted or not and however long ago, the very fact of being on the list was evidence of your permanent distinction from real football lovers. The formula was in place: the nineteenth century's 'dangerous offender', plus the all-purpose concept of 'risk', plus New Labour's somewhat casual approach to old-fashioned values such as legality. Ban anyone on the list from buying a ticket, entering a football ground or boarding certain trains. Perhaps they should spend certain weekends on house arrest, their passports confiscated. But this very episodic character of the problem weakens its essentialism: how could a real monster be so harmless in the months between European fixtures?

Sexual paedophiles are purer candidates for monster status. The July 2000 murder of eight-year-old Sarah Payne led to the *News of the World* 'crusade' (its word), a classic text of monster-making. The 23 July front page reads: 'NAMED SHAMED. There are 110,000 child sex offenders in Britain … one for every square mile. The murder of Sarah Payne has proved police monitoring of these perverts is not enough. So we are revealing WHO they are and WHERE they are … starting today.' The lists of names and the rows of photos reflect what the paper assumes and constructs as the primeval public anxiety: 'DOES A MONSTER LIVE NEAR YOU?' Then: 'WHAT TO DO IF THERE IS A PERVERT ON YOUR DOORSTEP.'

Many obvious and worrying issues were soon raised: how the list was constructed (partly from Scout Association records: *Scouting Out the Beasts,* the paper explains, although this claim was denied by the Scouts); how downloading child porn or the seduction of a 14-year-old schoolboy by his mid-30s female teacher belong to the same category as the sexual murder of a child; the dangers of vigilantism and lynch mobs; the counter-productive effect of driving already monitored offenders underground; the media's own freedom to publish.

There is another less obvious issue: the ease with which the moral discourse of evil, sin, monstrosity and perversion is coupled with the

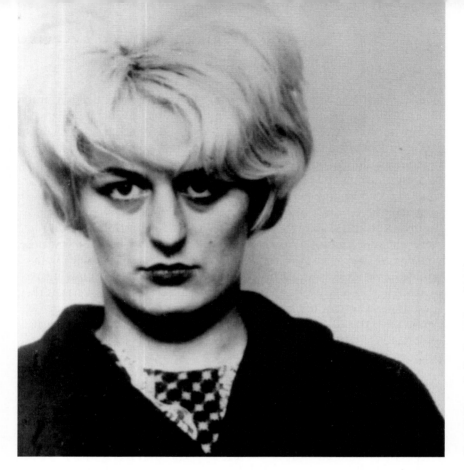

Myra Hindley – Credit: Camera Press Digital

medical model of sickness, pathology and untreatability. 'THEIR EVIL IS INCURABLE SAYS CRIME EXPERT' was another *News of the World* headline. But how can the morally blameworthy free agent also be the determined creature who lacks all freedom of choice? One answer is simple: the essence and permanence of being a 'paedophile' is guaranteed by *both* extreme (and untenable) versions of these opposite causal theories.

But all these objections sound irrelevant and self-indulgent compared with the personal tragedies themselves, the true horror of a child's death under any such circumstances and our own primeval identification with victim and family. The liberal critique of *News of the World* rhetoric is too easy; this type of monster-making has almost become ironic self-parody. The critique remains ineffectual as long as it treats with contempt the audience's feelings of horror and insecurity that lie behind the kitsch.

Go back, though, to amnesties or early mass releases of political prisoners, whether in Northern Ireland, South Africa or Israel. Liberals expect these publics to show an astonishing degree of tolerance. Back on their streets are people who have bombed buses, shopping malls, cafés or pubs, killing many innocent people at a time, a scale of devastation way beyond any paedophile murder. Yet under the vague slogans of 'reconciliation' and 'living together' or to preserve the shakiest of 'peace agreements', we expect ordinary people (including direct victims) to act with total political altruism.

At these moments, the voice of liberalism and human rights sounds very elitist. It takes little for generals, civil servants, politicians and lawyers to negotiate with ex-monsters. The personal lives of victims, survivors and their families demand much more. The South African TRC heard the story of Matthew Kondile, killed by the infamous Dirk Coetzee, one of the most savage leaders of the South African police death squads. Mrs Kondile refuses to forgive him. Mandela and Tutu, she says, can forgive because they live 'vindicated lives'. But: 'In my life nothing, not a single thing has changed since my son was burnt by barbarians. Nothing. Therefore I cannot forgive.'

This issue of *Index*, however, deals with other forms of monster-making where only human rights values should apply and no special sensitivity is needed to the private lives behind the public deals. Besides the specific renewal of the deep prejudice against Gypsies, there is the general media and public crusade against immigrants, asylum seekers and refugees. This crusade is fully synchronised with the government's populist 'policy' of doing everything possible to let as few outsiders into the country as possible (and criminalising many in the process). This not only runs against national economic self-interest but ignores the plight of millions of wretched people throughout the world. That a social democratic government has succeeded, after the whole of the last century, in making 'asylum seekers' and 'refugees' into monster words is almost unbelievable. ❏

Stanley Cohen *is professor of sociology at the London School of Economics.* Moral Panics and Folk Devils *(Blackwell) was published in 1972. His new book,* States of Denial: Knowing About Atrocities and Suffering *will be published by Polity Press in November this year.*

NOAM CHOMSKY

States of concern

The end of the Cold War necessitated new enemies. Enter the 'rogue state'

The concept of 'rogue state' plays a pre-eminent role today in policy planning and analysis. The ongoing Iraq crisis is only one example. Washington and London declared Iraq a 'rogue state', a threat to its neighbours and to the entire world, an 'outlaw nation' led by a reincarnation of Hitler who must be contained by the guardians of the world order, the United States and its British 'junior partner', to adopt the term ruefully employed by the British Foreign Office half a century ago.

The basic conception is that although the Cold War is over, the US still has the responsibility to protect the world – but from what? Plainly it cannot be from the threat of 'radical nationalism' – that is, unwillingness to submit to the will of the powerful. Such ideas are only fit for internal planning documents, not the general public. From the early 1980s, it was clear the conventional technique for mass mobilisation was losing its effectiveness: the appeal to JFK's 'monolithic and ruthless conspiracy', Reagan's 'evil empire'. New enemies were needed.

At home, fear of crime – particularly drugs – was stimulated by 'a variety of factors that have little or nothing to do with crime itself' the National Criminal Justice Commission concluded, including media practices and 'the role of government and private industry in stoking citizen fear', 'exploiting latent racial tension for political purpose', with racial bias in enforcement and sentencing that is devastating black communities, creating a 'racial abyss' and putting 'the nation at risk of a social catastrophe'. The results have been described by criminologists as 'the American Gulag', 'the new American Apartheid', with African Americans now a majority of prisoners for the first time in US history,

Anti-NATO Demonstrations in Belgrade, April 1999 – Credit:
Stefan Filipovic/Camera Press Digital

imprisoned at well over seven times the rate of whites, completely out of
the range of arrest rates, which themselves target blacks far out of
proportion to drug use or trafficking.

Abroad, the threats were to be 'international terrorism', 'Hispanic narcotraffickers' and, most serious of all, 'rogue states'. A secret 1995 study of the Strategic Command, which is responsible for the strategic nuclear arsenal, outlines the basis thinking. Released through the Freedom of Information Act, the study, *Essentials of Post-Cold War Deterrence*, 'shows how the United States shifted its deterrent strategy from the defunct Soviet Union to so-called rogue states such as Iraq, Libya, Cuba and North Korea', AP reports. The study advocates that the US exploits its nuclear arsenal to portray itself as 'irrational and vindictive if its vital interests are attacked'. That 'should be a part of the national persona we project to all adversaries', particularly the 'rogue states'. 'It hurts to portray ourselves as too fully rational and cool-headed', let alone committed to such silliness as international law and treaty obligations. 'The fact that some elements' of the US government 'may appear to be potentially "out of control" can be beneficial to creating and reinforcing fears and doubts within the minds of an adversary's decision makers'.

The report resurrects Nixon's 'madman theory': our enemies should recognise that we are crazed and unpredictable, with extraordinary destructive force at our command, so they will bend to our will in fear. The concept was apparently devised in Israel in the 1950s by the governing Labour Party, whose leaders 'preached in favour of acts of madness', Prime Minister Moshe Sharett records in his diary, warning that 'we will go crazy' [*nishtagea*] if crossed, a 'secret weapon' aimed in part against the US, not considered sufficiently reliable at the time.

In the hands of the world's sole superpower, which regards itself as an outlaw state and is subject to few constraints from elites within, that stance poses no small problem for the world.

Libya was a favourite choice as 'rogue state' from the earliest days of the Reagan administration. Vulnerable and defenceless, it is a perfect punching bag when needed: for example, in 1986, when the first bombing in history orchestrated for prime-time TV was used by the Great Communicator's speech writers to muster support for Washington's terrorist forces attacking Nicaragua, on grounds that the 'archterrorist' Qaddafi 'has sent US$400 million and an arsenal of weapons and advisors into Nicaragua to bring his war home to the United States', which was then exercising its right of self-defence against the armed attack of the Nicaraguan rogue state.

Immediately after the Berlin Wall fell, ending any resort to the Soviet threat, the Bush administration submitted its annual call to Congress for a huge Pentagon budget. It explained that 'In a new era, we foresee that our military power will remain an essential underpinning of the global balance, but ... the more likely demands for the use of our military forces may not involve the Soviet Union and may be in the third world, where new capabilities and approaches may be required', as 'when President Reagan directed US naval and air forces to return to [Libya] in 1986' to bombard civilian urban targets, guided by the goal of 'contributing to an international environment of peace, freedom and progress within which our democracy – and other free nations – can flourish'. The primary threat we face is the 'growing technological sophistication' of the third world. We must therefore strengthen 'the defence industrial base' – aka high-tech industry – creating incentives 'to invest in new facilities and equipment as well as in research and development'. And we must maintain intervention forces, particularly those targeting the Middle East, where the 'threats to our interests' that have required direct military engagement 'could not be laid at the Kremlin's door' – contrary to endless fabrication, now put to rest. As had occasionally been recognised in earlier years, sometimes in secret, the 'threat' is now conceded officially to be indigenous to the region, the 'radical nationalism' that has always been a primary concern, not only in the Middle East.

At that time, the 'threats to our interests' could not be laid at Iraq's door either. Saddam was then a favoured friend and trading partner. His status changed only a few months later, when he misinterpreted US willingness to allow him to modify the border with Kuwait by force as authorisation to take over the country – or from the perspective of the Bush administration, to duplicate what the US had just done in Panama.

Since then, Iraq has displaced Iran and Libya as the leading 'rogue state'. Others have never entered the ranks. Perhaps the most relevant case is Indonesia, which shifted from enemy to friend when General Suharto took power in 1965, presiding over an enormous slaughter that elicited great satisfaction in the West. Since then Suharto was 'our kind of guy' as the Clinton administration described him, while carrying out murderous aggression and endless atrocities against his own people – killing 10,000 Indonesians just in the 1980s, according to the personal testimony of 'our guy', who wrote that 'the corpses were left lying around as a form of shock therapy'. In December 1975, the UN

Security Council unanimously ordered Indonesia to withdraw its invading forces from East Timor 'without delay' and called upon 'all states to respect the territorial integrity of East Timor as well as the inalienable right of its people to self-determination'. The US responded by (secretly) increasing shipments of arms to the aggressors; Carter accelerated the arms flow once again as the attack reached near-genocidal levels in 1978.

The concept 'rogue state' is highly nuanced. Thus Cuba qualifies as a leading 'rogue state' because of its alleged involvement in international terrorism, but the US does not fall into the category despite its terrorist attacks against Cuba for close to 40 years. Cuba was a 'rogue state' when its military forces were in Angola, backing the government against South African attacks supported by the US. South Africa, in contrast, was not a rogue state then, nor during the Reagan years, when it caused over US$60 billion in damage and 1.5 million deaths in neighbouring states according to a UN commission, not to speak of events at home – and with ample US/UK support.

The criteria are fairly clear: a 'rogue state' is not simply a criminal state, but one that defies the orders of the powerful – who are, of course, exempt. ❏

Noam Chomsky *is professor of linguistics at Massachussetts Institute of Technology. His forthcoming book,* A New Generation Draws the Line: Kosovo, East Timor and the Standards of the West, *will be published by Verso, London/New York, later this year*
This is an edited version of the essay 'Rogue States' *in* Acts of Aggression *(Seven Stories Press, New York 1999)*

EDWARD SAID

Apocalypse now

The media in the West were happy to go along with their governments in bringing home to domestic audiences the righteous thrills of facing down a monster like Saddam Hussein. Far from offering criticism or dissent, they became an extension of the war against Iraq

It would be a mistake, I think, to reduce what is happening between Iraq and the United States simply to an assertion of Arab will and sovereignty versus US imperialism, which undoubtedly plays a central role in all this. However misguided, Saddam Hussein's cleverness is not that he is splitting the US from its allies (which he has not really succeeded in doing for any practical purpose) but that he is exploiting the astonishing clumsiness and failures of US foreign policy. Very few people, least of all Saddam himself, can be fooled into believing him to be the innocent victim of US bullying; most of what is happening to his unfortunate people, who are undergoing the most dreadful and unacknowledged suffering, is due in considerable degree to his callous cynicism – first of all, his indefensible and ruinous invasion of Kuwait, his persecution of the Kurds, his cruel egoism and pompous self-regard which persists in aggrandising himself and his regime at exorbitant and, in my opinion, totally unwarranted cost. It is impossible for him to plead the case for national security and sovereignty given his abysmal disregard of it in the case of Kuwait and Iran. Be that as it may, US vindictiveness has exacerbated the situation by imposing a regime of sanctions which, as Sandy Berger, the US national security adviser, has proudly said, is unprecedented for its severity in the whole world of history. It is believed that 567,000 Iraqi civilians have died since the Gulf War, mostly as a result of disease, malnutrition and deplorably poor medical care. Agricultue and industry are at a total standstill. This is unconscionable, of course, and for this the brazen inhumanity of US policymakers is also very largely to blame. But we must not forget that Saddam is feeding that inhumanity quite deliberately in order to dramatise the opposition between the US and the rest of the Arab world; having provoked a crisis with the US (or the United Nations dominated by the US), he at first dramatised the unfairness of the sanctions. But by continuing it, the issue has changed and has become his non-compliance, and the terrible effects of the sanctions have been marginalised. Still the underlying causes of an Arab/US crisis remain. A careful analysis of that crisis is imperative.

The US has always opposed any sign of Arab nationalism or independence, partly for its own imperial reasons and partly because its unconditional support for Israel requires it to do so. Since the 1973 war, and despite the brief oil embargo, Arab policy up to and including the peace process has tried to circumvent or mitigate that hostility by appealing to the US for help, by 'good' behaviour, by willingness to make peace with Israel. Yet mere compliance with the wishes of the US can produce nothing except occasional words of approbation for leaders who appear 'moderate': Arab policy was never backed up with coordination, or collective pressure, or fully agreed upon goals. Instead, each leader tried to make separate arrangements both with the US and with Israel, none of which produced very much except escalating demands and a constant refusal by the US to exert any meaningful pressure on Israel. The more extreme Israeli policy becomes, the more likely the US has been to support it, and the less respect it has for the large mass of Arab peoples whose future and well-being are mortgaged to illusory hopes embodied, for instance, in the Oslo accords.

Moreover, a deep gulf separates Arab culture and civilisation from the US and, in the absence of any collective Arab information and cultural policy, the notion of an Arab people with traditions, cultures and identities of their own is simply inadmissible in the US. Arabs are dehumanised, they are seen as violent irrational terrorists always on the lookout for murder and bombing outrages. The only Arabs worth doing business with are compliant leaders, businessmen and military people whose arms purchases (the highest per capita in the world) are helping the US economy keep afloat. Beyond that, there is no feeling at all, for instance, for the dreadful suffering of the Iraqi people whose identity and existence have simpley been lost sight of in the present situation. This morbid, obsessional fear and hatred of the Arabs has been a constant theme in US foreign policy since WWII. In some way, also, anything positive about the Arabs is seen in the US as a threat to Israel. In this respect, pro-Israeli American Jews, traditional Orientalists and military hawks have played a devastating role. Moral opprobrium is heaped on Arab states as it is on no others. Turkey, for example, has been conducting a campaign against the Kurds for several years, yet nothing is heard about this in the US. Israel occupies territory illegally for 30 years, violates the Geneva conventions at will, conducts invasions, terrorist attacks and assassinations against Arabs, and still the US vetoes every sanction against it in the United Nations. Syria, Sudan, Libya, Iraq are classified as 'rogue states'. Sanctions against them are far harsher than against any other countries in the history of US foreign policy. And still the US expects that its own foreign policy agenda ought to prevail despite its hostility to the collective Arab agenda. In the case of Iraq, a number of further extenuations make the US even more repressive. Burning in the collective US unconscious is a puritanical zeal decreeing the sternest possible attitude towards anyone deemed to be an unregenerate sinner. This clearly guided US policy towards the native American Indians, who were first demonised, then portrayed as wasteful savages, then exterminated, their tiny remnant confined to reservations and concentration camps. This almost religious anger fuels a judgmental attitude that has no place at all in international politics, but for the US it is a central tenet of its worldwide behaviour. Punishment is conceived in apocalyptic terms. During the Vietnam War, a leading general advocated – and almost achieved – the goal of bombing the enemy into the Stone Age. The same view prevailed during the Gulf War in 1991. Sinners are meant to be condemned terminally, with the utmost cruelty regardless of whether or not they suffer the cruellest agonies. The notion of 'justified' punishment for Iraq is now uppermost in the minds of most US consumers of news, and with that goes an almost orgiastic delight in the power used to confront Iraq in the Gulf.

Forgotten in all this is that the US has all the terror weapons known to humankind, is the only country to have used a nuclear bomb on civilians, and as recently as nine years ago dropped 66,000 tonnes of bombs on Iraq. As the only country involved in this crisis that has never had to fight a war on its own soil, it is easy for the US and its mostly brainwashed citizens to speak in apocalyptic terms. Unfortunately, the dictates of raw power are very severe and, for a weak state like Iraq,

Samawa, Iraq, August 2000. Damage caused by two nights of US and British bombing. Several civilians were injured and two killed. Credit: PA/EPA

overwhelming. Certainly, US misuse of the sanctions to strip Iraq of everything, including any possibility for security, is monstrously sadistic. In addition, the US and its clients – eg the unpleasant and racist Richard Butler, who says openly that Arabs have a different notion of truth from the rest of the world – have made it clear that even if Iraq is completely reduced militarily to the point where it is no longer a threat to its neighbours (which is now the case) the real goal of the sanctions is to topple Saddam Hussein's government. According to the US government, very little that Iraq can do short of Saddam's resignation or death will produce a lifting of sanctions. Finally, we should not for a moment forget that quite apart from its foreign policy interest, Iraq has now become a domestic issue whose repercussions on issues unrelated to oil or the Gulf are very important. Bill Clinton's personal crises – the campaign-funding scandals, a trial for sexual harassment, his various legislative and domestic failures – required him to look strong, determined and 'presidential' somewhere else, and where but in the Gulf against Iraq had he so ready-made a foreign devil to set off his blue-eyed strength to full advantage. Moreover, the increase in military expenditure for new investments in electronic 'smart' weaponry, more sophisticated aircraft and mobile forces for the worldwide projection of US power are perfectly suited for display and use in the Gulf, where the likelihood of visible casualities (actually suffering Iraqi civilians) is extremely small, and where the new military technology can be put through its paces most attractively. For reasons that need restating here, the media is particularly happy to go along with the government in bringing home to domestic customers the wonderful excitement of US self-righteousness, the proud flag-waving, the 'feel-good' sense that 'we' are facting down a monstrous dictator. Far from analysis and calm reflection, the media exists mainly to derive its mission from the government, not to produce a corrective or any dissent. The media, in short, is an extension of the war against Iraq.

The saddest aspect of the whole thing is that Iraqi civilians seem condemned to additional suffering and protracted agony. Neither their government nor that of the US is inclined to ease the daily pressure on them, and the probability that only they will pay for the crisis is extremely high. ❏

Edward Said is professsor of English and comparative literature at Columbia University. He was formerly a member of the Palestinian National Council and is the author of many books, among them Orientalism *and* Covering Islam. *His most recent book is* The End of the Peace Process: Oslo and After *(Pantheon, New York).* Reflections on Exile and other essays *(Harvard University Press) is due in February 2001*
This article was first published in Arabic in Al Hayat, *London. This edited version is from* Acts of Aggression *(Seven Stories Press, New York, 1999)*

JEREMY HARDING

Double indemnity

Would-be refugees frequently suffer a twofold contempt: they are the object of abuse in their own country – for which reason they leave it – only to find that their reputation as monsters has preceded their arrival in the place where they seek asylum

When José Bové, the Larzac sheep farmer, ran a bulldozer through the site of a McDonald's in the south of France in August 1999, he was regarded by many of his compatriots as a giant-slayer. A significant section of French opinion sees McDonald's as a monster in the vanguard of globalisation – a US monster, crushing the traditions of the French Republic, and *la France profonde*, underfoot. '*Non à la McDomination*' was one of the slogans chanted at Bové's trial this summer. But the mother of all burger joints is too often linked with another, insistent presence in French life: that of the foreign migrant. Both are seen as frightening symptoms of a shrinking world in which old, indigenous virtues become soluble and eventually wash away. '*Non à McDonald's, non à la mosquée*' is the cry from those who want international capital and immigrants from poorer countries like Morocco and Algeria turned back at the border.

This desire for a strong posture at the margins of national, or federal, sovereignty is understandable. It is, after all, only about the wish to determine what happens on the inside – a wish that gets stronger as the ability to exercise control seems to diminish. The difficulty is that a European Union with an impregnable single border may not be realistic; or that, if it is, it can only be achieved at an unacceptable price.

'Fortress Europe' is the shorthand for the kind of extravagance that it involves. Aside from the hard costs of keeping out immigrants – fortification, surveillance, military and police deployment – there is an ideological price to pay, for under the new rules of globalisation, liberalism within one political entity may work no better than socialism

Refugees in guest house, Dover – Credit: Cecilia Choi

in one country did. And the defensive insulation of a liberal society founded more than ever on conspicuous economic privilege may be as unseemly as the savage wars for geopolitical influence that the West waged during the superpower era. It may even corrupt the thing it is intended to defend, just as the conflicts of the Cold War in Africa, Latin America and Asia corrupted many cherished liberal nostrums in the 'free world' at the time. It was these proxy wars that turned liberalism into a dirty word.

In more practical terms, capital has been crossing international borders for many years; and since the late 1980s it has enjoyed virtual freedom of movement in most parts of the world, with decisive results for citizens in states that are thousands of miles from a multinational HQ or the terminal of a big currencies trader. Yet plenty of Europeans who argue for the unrestricted movement of money and goods are keenly opposed to freer movements of human beings across international boundaries: you could characterise this view as '*Oui à McDonald's, non à la mosquée*'. It takes no account of the possibility that, with capital scudding around the world at extraordinary speeds, people may begin to move in larger numbers than they do already.

According to the International Organisation for Migration, there are around 150 million people living outside their country of origin – less than three per cent of the world's population. Of these, an even smaller proportion resort to illegal means of entry into other states. They are, nonetheless, the people who alarm us most when we fall into our dark dream about the intruder. It is, of course, a dream about ruptured sovereignty. Most citizens, like governments, believe that the outer edges of their states should be reinforced to keep illegal migrants out. But in an internationalised economy with growing possibilities for people to move around, it is not consensus within states that matters so much as consensus across them. The members of a rich nation, or a federation, may respect its borders, yet if even a small number of people beyond those borders see them only as a barrier to safety or prosperity, then they are no longer a matter of consensus, but of dispute. Disputes over borders are also disputes over the extent of sovereignty. It's not surprising that we conceive of the people who try to breach the boundaries of wealthy states and unions as monsters.

Asylum seekers have never been popular but in the last ten years or so, their 'image problem' – in a world where image marketing is paramount – has got very much worse. In some parts of the British press, they are no longer people in distress, but 'human sewage' (the quotation is from a rabble-rousing *Dover Express* editorial in 1998). Two important changes account for the new notoriety of the asylum seeker. First, since the end of the Cold War, growing numbers of people in the remains of the Soviet Union and eastern Europe have been economically marginalised or become prey to a 'well-founded fear of being persecuted'. They have headed west, with the result that countries like Britain now find themselves playing host to higher numbers of asylum seekers than they have had to deal with for half a century. Second, since the mid-1980s, Britain and others have been at pains to close off most legal forms of entry to asylum seekers – by means of visa requirements and stiff penalties for carriers whose passengers arrive without proper documentation. Because the increase in numbers has coincided with exclusionary measures, more and more asylum seekers have been thrown back on clandestine entry in order to lodge their claims (*Index* 3/1994).

In the process, they have come to depend on 'human traffickers', organised crime rings or more informal networks of people who can help them to safety. Such networks, in the view of governments and journalists, are also composed of monsters – ruthless profiteers who think nothing of leading clients to their deaths, having first extorted large sums of money from them. This is a very partial truth. 'Human traffickers' come in a variety of shapes and sizes. Organised crime has undoubtedly profited from people in need. In Italy, during the 1990s, the Sacra Corona Unita, one of the four Mafia agglomerates, aided and abetted the Albanian syndicates that ran refugees and illegal migrants across the Otranto Channel into Puglia. The Chinese 'snakeheads' are said to keep illegal migrants in a life of semi-slavery in their destinations, until they or their families have paid the full cost of passage. Meanwhile, thousands of clandestine migrants from eastern Europe have wound up as unwilling participants in the sex trade a few hundred miles west.

Yet the evidence suggests that many of the individuals and groups who traffic human beings from one place to another are careful of their safety and correct in their dealings with them. This is a business, after all – one which has burgeoned in proportion as the West has tried to cut off access to outsiders – and only the most powerful crime rings handling the most desperate people can afford a reputation for complete unscrupulousness.

There is no solace here for asylum seekers, however. Their image is tarnished by their association with illegality, racketeering and disregard for sovereign borders, even though Paragraph 1, Article 31 of the 1951 Convention Relating to the Status of Refugees recognises that they may be obliged to use illicit means of entry into a safe country and requires that host countries 'shall not impose penalties' on that account. Asylum seekers are also believed to be 'flooding' Britain. It is true that the figures have been high – almost 90,000 asylum claims were lodged in 1999 – but since the early 1990s, the number of refugees worldwide has hovered between 13 and 19 million. The EU member states take in only a fraction of this total.

To invent the asylum seeker as a predatory figure we have had to convince ourselves that refugees are always threatening to overwhelm us. This, in turn, has meant forgetting, or setting aside, the history of the last century, the 1920s and 30s in particular, when comparable numbers of people were on the move in Europe. We have also forgotten that, historically, asylum seekers have often had to lie and dissimulate in order to get to a safe country – an amnesia that allows us to make their journeys even more dangerous than they might be.

But there is another, alarming side to the fabrication of this enemy within and without, already present, yet always knocking at the door. Hannah Arendt pointed it out in *The Origins of Totalitarianism*. It has to do with the fact that refugees are often the focus of a twofold contempt, first in their country of origin and then in the place where they claim asylum. For Arendt – who was writing about the 'denationalisations' of the 1920s and 30s – there was no doubt that states could project their prejudices. She believed it was a simple matter for a totalitarian regime to ensure that the people it turned into outcasts were received as outcasts wherever they went. She refers to an extract from a circular put out in 1938 by the German Ministry of Foreign Affairs to its diplomatic staff abroad: 'The influx of Jews in all parts of the world invokes the opposition of the native population and thereby forms the best propaganda for the German Jewish policy ... The poorer and therefore more burdensome the immigrating Jew is to the country absorbing him, the stronger the reaction of the country.' Arendt felt this was more or less what happened. 'Those whom persecution had called undesirable,' she wrote, 'became the *indésirables* of Europe.'

Sweeping, certainly, but her remarks catch the drift of the refugee's central misfortune: that he or she is shuttled along a continuum of abuse that begins when a proportion of its people are accused of 'subversions of brotherhood and unity', as many ethnic Albanians were in the former Yugoslavia, and persists when a local newspaper a thousand miles away starts talking about 'human sewage'. Whenever we think of asylum seekers as a nuisance, or worse, we can be sure that someone else reached the same conclusion about them in their country of origin.

The question is how many monsters we can afford to have in a world where it has become harder for any state, or major city, to keep the rest of the world at a remove. Even if we don't care for McDonald's, we may have to put up with it. As for asylum seekers, we could do worse than welcome them. The alternative is the patrolled perimeter and the idyll of purity that ends in decay. ❏

Jeremy Harding is a senior editor at the London Review of Books, *where parts of this article first appeared. His latest book is* The Uninvited: Refugees at the Rich Man's Gate *(Profile and the LRB)*

LALA MEREDITH-VULA

Bathers

East European Roma women made their appearance in London in spring 2000, first to beg, then bewilder and finally enrage their puzzled hosts. Rumours of their rapacity here, and their wealth back home were fanned by reporters into a campaign of disgust, intensified by charges that Roma mothers were exploiting their children to prey on good-natured passers-by so as to increase their takings. Ignorant of English, the women went unconcernedly about their business until the evil hour when they collided with outright hostility or police arrest.

From 1994 to 1996, Sarajevo-born Lala Meredith-Vula photographed Roma females, aged from nine months to 90 years, washing themselves at an unrestored Ottoman bath-house on the Albania-Montenegro border. Visits to the Turkish bath were one of the few opportunities for women to socialise in a secluded, Moslem society. By the mid-1990s, however, the bathers were the poorest of the poor – Roma, the homeless and others with no access to bathing facilities. ❏

Anglo-Albanian artist **Lala Meredith-Vula** *exhibited in Damien Hirst's 'Freeze' show and represented Albania in the 1999 Venice Biennale. Her new work will be shown at London's Imperial War Museum in October 2001.*

TAHIR ABBAS

Images of Islam

No one loves a monster like the British press – and Islam is always there to hand when the need arises and the time is ripe

Islam has been feared and loathed by the West since it first made its appearance in Europe in the eighth century – within a century of its creation in the deserts of Arabia. Centuries later, Richard the Lionheart of England placed the nobility and chivalry of Saladin, his opponent in the Crusade to recover the Holy Places of Jerusalem, above that of his own side. Then as now, it made little difference to the popular perception of Christianity's only rival.

Muslims are the largest religious minority in Britain, around 55% of them from the Indian subcontinent with the majority settled in south-eastern England. It is on the latter community that Islamophobia is dominantly visited. While the term Islamophobia, coined to express the mix of fear and dread that characterises western attitudes to Islam, is of relatively recent date, modern anti-Muslim sentiment, as expressed in the British press, for instance, is simply one version of a well-established tradition more or less coterminous with the first confrontation of the two communities all those centuries ago

Throughout their mutual history, the powers of western Europe, fearing contact with Muslims could lead to conversions to the new religion, demonised Islam and its believers in the interests of whipping up Christian resistance among a population little inclined to go to war with the invader whom they found little worse than their present lords and masters and, often, rather more civilised than less. Then as now, the representation of 'the other' in a negative light legitimised existing power structures and served as propaganda in the long centuries of the battle against Islam. Spain was occupied and ruled by its Muslim conquerors for seven centuries: Granada did not finally fall to the Christian rulers Ferdinand and Isabella until 1492. The armies of the

Turkish sultan were last at the gates of Vienna as late as 1683. Perceptions and conceptions of Islam in the West have had plenty of time to mature.

Although there have been times of mutual learning and understanding, these are isolated moments in the general climate of ignorance, conflict and demonisation in which it has been easier to accept the most outrageous of the myths: Muslims were – and still are – defined as barbaric, ignorant, closed-minded semi-citizens, or maddened terrorists and intolerant religious zealots.

Today's Islamophobia feeds on history to fill out its stereotypes, but it also has features that stem from more recent narratives such as colonialism, immigration and racism. The Runnymede Trust, a British funding body, identified seven features of Islamophobia: Muslim cultures are monolithic; substantially different from others; implacable and threatening; Muslims use their faith for political or military advantage; their criticism of western cultures and societies is rejected out of hand; fear of Islam is linked to racist hostility to immigration; Islamophobia itself is assumed to be 'natural' and therefore unproblematic.

The term 'fundamentalism', first applied to Islam after the Iranian revolution in 1979, added to the existing wealth of historical prejudice and heralded a new, particularly adversarial phase in Muslim-Christian relations. As represented by the media, 'Islamic fundamentalists' became the 'true' Muslims', and all Muslims were Islamic fundamentalists. The *Observer* referred to 'the phenomenon of the new, or rather very old Islam, the dangerous fundamentalism revived by the ayatollahs and their admirers as a device, indistinguishable from a weapon, for running a modern state'. The article referred to the 'new Islamic states' as 'little more than intolerant, bloody and finally incompetent animations of the Holy Book. Comparisons between the Qur'an and Hitler's *Mein Kampf* referred to the chopping off of hands and gouging out of eyes, concluding that there was 'more blood and stupidity than glamour in the theocracy of the Sons of the Prophet'.

The period following the Rushdie affair in Britain (1989) and the Gulf War (1990-1991) gave the press and its cartoonists – the broadsheet 'quality' papers as much as the tabloids – their head with scarcely a voice raised in protest at images and comments that were racist and Islamophobic, and deeply offensive to Muslims at a time when they were soft targets for vicious lampoons that took advantage of their weakness.

Particularly when the groups concerned were largely unrepresented in the mainstream press and silenced by the lack of any alternative voice.

"HE SAYS HE WASN'T GETTING ANYWHERE IN THE OTHER BRITISH PARLIAMENT!"

Credit: Sun, 1992

Credit: Today, 1992

In the *Sun*, Neil Kinnock, then leader of the Labour Party in opposition, seeks to improve his political fortunes. *Today*'s cartoon is self-explanatory. Both images imply a sense of the enemy within: Muslims are infiltrating Britain and plan to overtake government from inside the borders of Britain. As do those that home in on immigration.

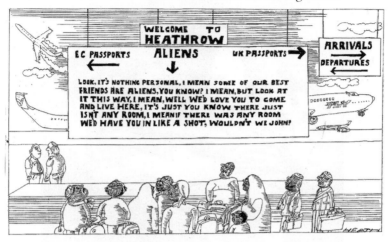

Credit: Independent, 1991

Credit: Sun, 1992

The *Independent* cartoonist criticises the apparently open government policy on immigration and asylum, while the *Sun* puts Asian immigrants at the bottom of the social heap.

Credit: The Times, 1992

The Times cartoon with an article by Bernard Levin headlined 'Prayers of Poison' fills the Indian subcontinent with violence, confrontation and intolerance for which Islamic fanaticism is to blame. ❏

Tahir Abbas *is co-author, with Alex Hall and Nusrat Shaheen, of* The Demonisation of Muslims in the British Press: Islamophobes, Fundamentalists and Political Cartoons, *a report funded by the Runnymede Trust. He works at the Centre for Research in Ethnic Relations at the University of Warwick, UK*

cheltenham *festival of*
literature

IN ASSOCIATION WITH
THE INDEPENDENT

13-22 october *2000*

This October the Festival reaches out to the last frontier with a ten-day exploration of space and literature looking at the ways in which place, location and identity influence writers. In more than two hundred compelling events, writers from across the globe come to Cheltenham to reveal literary locations, break boundaries and take us on journeys around the world and into their work.

Book It! offers children an unmissable annual feast of activities, adventures and the chance to meet exciting authors from **Joan Aiken** to **Martin Jarvis**. *Voices Off*, with distinctive events at friendly town centre venues, has a dashing array of poets and performers, singers and storytellers, troubadours and talkers appearing everywhere from cafés and pubs to bars and on board a bus.

Brochure Hotline Tel: 01242 237377

Booking Hotline Tel: 01242 227979

Write to: Literature Festival Box Office, Town Hall, Imperial Square, Cheltenham, Gloucestershire, GL50 1QA

Visit: www.cheltenhamfestivals.co.uk

Thomas Keneally
Jostein Gaarder
Doris Lessing
Jeanette Winterson
David Starkey
Michael Heseltine
Ronald Blythe
Gitta Sereny
Susan Greenfield
Miranda Seymour
Hermione Lee
Roy Porter
Edward Said
Prunella Scales

Bill Bryson
Willy Russell
Martin Bell
Andrew Motion
Adrian Noble
Richard Eyre
Frank Kermode
George Walden
Norman Davies
Leon Brittan
Max Hastings
Roy Strong
Frederic Raphael
Redmond O'Hanlon

…are just some of the three hundred writers appearing at the Literature Festival 2000.

ROY GREENSLADE

Monstermania and tabloid antics

There's no one can point the finger and whip up a mob faster than the press when it puts its mind to it. Cry foul, but don't demand tabloid silence

Surely everyone in Britain agrees: Saddam Hussein is a warmongering, bloodthirsty despot; Slobodan Milosevic is a racist tyrant; and Moors murderer Myra Hindley is an evil woman who should be locked away in solitary and fed on bread and water for the rest of her natural life.

According to newspaper lore – resting for its justification on the views of those mythical men on the Clapham omnibus and Wigan Pier – they are self-evidently 'monsters'.

Should you require a definition, monsters are people who, because of their abominable behaviour, cannot be redeemed. They have forfeited all rights to be treated as human beings.

Now, I don't intend to debate the merits and demerits of arguments about whether the above trio deserve to have been demonised and dehumanised. For our purposes, the significant point is that all three, for different reasons, are classic examples of media-manufactured monsters. At the mention of their surnames alone, the reactions of tabloid readers across Britain can be predicted. They are beyond the pale. Hanging would be too good for them. Just as important, anyone who shows even the least understanding or compassion for them is either mad or bad, or both.

Joining the trio in the tabloids' Hall of Infamy from the end of July was a group rather than an individual: the Paedophile. This media monster, long in the manufacturing process, rolled off the assembly line as a finished product following the *News of the World*'s controversial

'Name and Shame' campaign.

However, the Paedophile, by the very nature of its rather loose definition, is a disturbing extension of the media monstrosity phenomenon. Before we look closely at it, we require some history and context.

The first requirement of media monsters is that they appeal to the prejudices of the majority, that by their acts or, on occasion, simply by their existence, they can be portrayed as separate, different and, if not demonstrably wicked, then certainly capable of wickedness.

Mythomaniac editors are, of course, aware of the prejudices of their readers and know exactly which buttons to push to stimulate outrage. They can then employ a battery of journalistic techniques – repetition, selective reporting, polemic, distortion, hyperbole, factual omission – to ensure that the person or group will be damned for ever more. All of this appeals, of course, to the emotions rather than the intellect, a crucial part of the process. From the moment of demonisation, papers must be sure that the monster will engender the correct knee-jerk reactions. It is therefore always the case that papers either play on pre-existing fears in society, or – in the case of creating foreign monsters – must show that they pose a threat to our way of life or the lives of Our Boys.

This reminds us that there are various categories of media monster and it is instructive to review them:

● **Foreign dictators** Along with the two named above, there have been Argentina's General Galtieri, Romania's Nicolae Ceausescu, Uganda's Idi Amin and Libya's Colonel Qaddafi. Robert Mugabe of Zimbabwe is well down the production line. Oddly, Kenya's arap Moi hasn't even entered the factory.

● **Domestic murderers** Hindley's partner, Ian Brady; the Yorkshire Ripper, Peter Sutcliffe; the Black Panther, Donald Neilson; multiple murderer Dennis Nilsen; the boys who killed James Bulger; and police killer Harry Roberts.

● **Celebrities** Fatty Arbuckle and, to an extent, Charlie Chaplin, were early examples. Paul Robeson's communism was enough to make him a monster in McCarthyite America. Gary Glitter, regularly headlined as a 'pervert', is the most recent celebrity monster.

● **Immigrants** Here is the first use of the group as monster. The Irish suffered media hostility from the 19th century on. Even the sainted cartoonist David Low, whose anti-Home Rule credentials were impeccable, caricatured the Irish as simian creatures, confessing that his drawings 'were composed of traditional Irish types of archaic burlesque with button noses, long upper lips and upside-down short "cutty pipes". The Jews suffered centuries of prejudice and were routinely referred to in contemptuous terms in the press a century ago. But they became media monsters in the 1930s when they were 'flooding' into Britain and again, after the war, when inaccurately accused of running black market activities at a time when they were killing British soldiers in Palestine. West Indians and Asians from India and Pakistan have been, at various times, cast in the role of monster. Of late, the Roma have suffered a similar fate, along with others from eastern Europe.

● **Muslims** Whether in Britain or outside, Arabs and Muslims generally been demonised at various key moments.

● **Political figures** Though the great political dramas of the 1970s and 80s have faded from the memory, for a while Vanessa Redgrave, Derek Hatton, Arthur Scargill, Ken Livingstone and Derek Robinson (Red Robbo) were given monster-style status. They have lost their monster tags now, but only because they have either lost their power to threaten the status quo, or acquiesced to it.

● **The IRA** Anyone connected to the IRA, as a member or in its political wing, Sinn Fein, was a media monster. The murderous Loyalist groups were never given the same kind of media treatment.

● **Paedophiles** The new monsters. It is interesting to recall that the first time a case of paedophilia made tabloid headline news, in 1951, it was conflated with a sexual preference which also made its post-war debut in the popular prints: homosexuality. These two have been linked ever since in the public imagination.

In 1952 the *Sunday Pictorial* published a series, entitled 'Evil Men', which was a direct offshoot of the disgraceful case of a priest who had abused the male pupils at the London Choir School, where he was headmaster. Over the following three years, the *Pictorial*, equating the man's illegal paedophile acts with homosexuality, campaigned to root out teachers who had been found guilty of homosexual offences.

In 1956, the *Daily Mirror*'s acerbic columnist Cassandra described the US entertainer Liberace as a 'deadly, winking, sniggering, snuggling, chromium-plated, scent-impregnated, luminous, quivering, giggling, fruit-flavoured, mincing, ice-covered heap of mother love' and an

Letter from a paedophile

I WILL NOT TELL YOU MY NAME. I have a senior managerial job, I support my local football team, I drink at my local pub, I look very normal. I am also a paedophile. I am attracted to young girls between the ages of six and nine and am one of approximately 0.01% of the adult male population of NW Europe. I will not, however, seek to justify my sexuality, just as I do not expect you to justify yours.

Yet we are part of western culture. Socrates, Plato, Byron, Lewis Carroll, Baden-Powell, Mark Twain, Charlie Chaplin and Gary Glitter are some of the better known paedophiles. There are as many paedophiles today as there were 150 years ago, so why do you vilify us now?

Contrary to popular myth, our relationships are based on consent rather than coercion. The child is always in control, and perfectly able to say 'no' as well as 'yes', but usually says 'maybe' and wants to do something else. Paedophiles love children and seek their company. They appreciate the beauty of children, and all the ones I know would never dream of hurting a child. On the contrary, we take care of them, listen to them (which is more than most adults do) and, let's face it, we're more interesting than their other friends. The myth of the child-raping monster is perpetuated by the child sex abuse industry.

Sexually motivated child murders in the UK have remained at less then four per year for the last ten years, yet children are guarded closer then ever. The recent hysteria generated by the British media is symptomatic of this new attitude, yet the truth does not support their arguments.

Mention the word paedophile today and we get lumped with rape, murder and worse. Marc Dutroux is always called a paedophile, but he is clinically diagnosed as a psychopath. When a man sexually assaults a girl he is called a paedophile, yet when the same man sexually assaults a woman he is a rapist. Abuse is abuse, rape is rape, and this is not what motivates paedophiles, just as it does not motivate others. We have morals, just as you do. I despise violent and sexual abuse of children, just as I condemn child labour. They're the same thing.

Children have sexuality, and you are afraid to admit this. Why do you want to prosecute friends and lovers along with rapists? Why are you afraid of what you do not want to understand? We will not go away and you cannot suppress us or ignore us. All we ask is rational dialogue and understanding as a way towards peaceful coexistence. We're nice people, really. ❏

De Buitenlander

This article was offered anonymously by an Index *subscriber* 'appalling ... terrifying man'. Much has been made of the fact that Liberace lied in court, denying he was a homosexual. (Since homosexuality was against the law, he would have been foolish to admit it.) Less attention has been paid to the fact that Cassandra lied as well: he claimed that he had not intended the imputation Liberace alleged (namely, that he was a homosexual). More to the point, by using the word 'terrifying', what Cassandra was doing was suggesting that Liberace was a threat to Britain. In other words, he was referring to the supposed nexus between the homosexual and the paedophile.

It is highly likely that this deliberate misconception, widely portrayed in popular paper articles, delayed the passage of legislation that decriminalised homosexuality. It certainly helped to foster the idea that one gave rise to the other. So potent has that media myth become that public attitudes have not really changed in the following 40 years.

As far as paedophilia is concerned, the term – which has only recently come into common use – has come to mean whatever newspapers have wanted it to mean. It has been extended in tabloid use to cover a whole range of activities – from abduction and murder to the viewing of pornography and indecent exposure – which has enlarged the number of possible offenders and, naturally, the number of possible 'monsters'.

But the widening of the net has also served to narrow the public debate and concealed an unpalatable truth: that most strictly paedophile activity is a form of incest, in which fathers – and, more usually, common-law stepfathers – force themselves on a child. But this uncomfortable fact does not fit with the press's refrain about the importance of family values, and conflicts with its desire to play on fears of the itinerant bogeyman who represents a potential threat to the life of every child. To run a campaign against the monster lurking in the home would probably cause a boycott of the paper.

The importance of the monster-manufacturing process is that it should strike a chord (usually of fear) in the public mind. But the creation of the paedophile monster is quite unlike every other category listed above. Most of them cannot be reached by the public. Those who can, such as immigrants, are, even if grudgingly, assimilated into society. Time heals. Irrational prejudice breaks down in the face of fact. Newspapers gradually wind down their absurd campaigns.

The difference with paedophiles is that they can be reached and,

NEWS
OF THE
WORLD

EDITOR'S
OFFICE

GONE
TO
LYNCH

MIKE TURNER

Credit: *Private Eye/Mike Turner*

given the nature of their crimes, are rarely forgiven. Newspapers will never cease their hostility. This is the monster for a millennium. This creates the greatest problem of all: what is to be done to or for the convicted child molester? Newspapers raise a hue and cry and leave it at that. Governments, fearing to take any radical action in the face of newspaper hostility, wash their hands of the problem.

In that sense, I understand the motives of the *News of the World*'s editor. Recognising a policy vacuum, she thought she was acting for the public good. But the device, manufacturing yet another monster, will surely prove counter-productive. Media monsters foment mobs. And mobs, as the paper discovered, are uncontrollable, producing monsters of their own. ❏

Roy Greenslade *is a journalist with the* Guardian, *London*

ANDRZEJ OSEKA

Fun conspiracy

In July this year, when the campaign for the Polish presidential election opened, Marcin Libicki, an MP from the Christian-People's Union, sent a letter to prospective candidates, asking: 'What is your attitude to the legalisation of so-called "homosexual marriages"?' 'What is your attitude to the possibility of homosexual couples adopting children?'

The right-wing dignified this letter as a patriotic act, justified by the gravity of the situation, since 'liberalism' was once again striking at Christian Europe and the Catholic family. The weekly *Niedziela* said: 'The declarations of organisations of homosexuals are growing ever more brazen and aggressive. In the cities of Europe they are staging spectacular marches of debauchery; they accuse the Holy Father of crimes; the memory of the victims of Auschwitz-Birkenau is dishonoured …'

At the beginning of July, two major gatherings met in Rome: a Polish Catholic 'Jubilee Year 2000' pilgrimage and the First 'World Gay Pride' Congress. On 8 July, a colourful parade of gays marched along the route, shouting 'We've conquered the Coliseum.' Pope John Paul II called the homosexual jamboree an 'affront to the Great Jubilee year 2000 and the values of the Christian City as the precious heart of the world's Catholics'. He recalled that, as the Catechism of the Catholic Church stresses, 'homosexual acts … are contrary to the natural law', although, as the Catechism also notes, 'a significant number of men and women have deeply seated homosexual inclinations and do not choose their homosexual condition'. Such persons, the pope recalled, must be 'treated with respect, sympathy and delicacy'.

The press – both Polish and worldwide – did not view the pope's comments as an appeal for sympathy, but as a subtext of disapproval. The Dutch gay organisation filed defamation charges against the pope for discrimination against sexual minorities. The charges were rejected on the grounds of 'papal immunity'.

The fact that gays had encroached on a Polish pilgrimage and tried to prosecute our 'Polish' pope set off alarm bells on the right. The newspaper *Zycie* on 14 July carried the headline, 'Homosexuals' strategy ever more reminiscent of Bolshevik methods and tactics'. The author, Piotr Semka, analyses the seditious means of the gay media: 'The truth is that homosexuals, who are extremely numerous in the media, advertising and show business, are able to put on mass events as symbolised by the Berlin "Love Parades". Officially, the Berlin event had no political nor sexual character but, in reality, it was the homosexuals who had the greatest influence on its style and atmosphere of erotic freedom. The parades in Rome and Berlin had the same purpose.'

Homosexuals hidden in the crowd, Semka suggests, are 'teaching each other to blaspheme. They eagerly make anti-Catholic alliances with Lutherans, Methodists, Jews. This is exactly like the Bolsheviks who, though weak, tried to take power by deceit.' They know how to 'draw the masses to themselves by an attractive vision of a pop-culture ideology of fun and games, looseness and moral freedom. It would appear that the world may be threatened at any moment with a totalitarianism in which the role of the One Party is taken by gay societies.'

A similar threat is portrayed by *Tygodnik* Solidarnosc, which carries the insignia of the trades union once headed by Lech Walesa. On 14 July, it carried an article by Marcin Przewozniak, entitled 'Homo invasion'. Here homosexuals are called simply 'sodomites' and 'perverts', whose 'street orgies have defiled Rome'. Przewozniak suggests that if one gives rights to homosexuals, paedophiles will be next, and then zoophiles will want recognition for a 'special union with a beloved goat'.

Marek Jurek, one of the most active politicians of the right, published in *Nasz Dziennik* a text entitled 'Homoliberalism has appeared on the banks of the Vistula'. Here, the author proposes his evidence: when a (female) journalist asked President Aleksander Kwasniewski (who is seeking a second term of office) his views on homosexual 'marriages' and adoptions, the president replied: 'These are normal people, and if they want to bring up children, let them do so!' The Catholic-Popular paper *Glos* (23 July) devoted two columns to Kwasniewski's programme of 'entrusting infants into the hands of effeminates, or persons wearing the fetters and skins of degenerates'. ❏

Andrzej Oseka, *art critic and columnist with* Gazeta Wyborcza, *contributed to the uncensored press from 1982 to 1989. Translated by Vera Rich*

IRENA MARYNIAK

Extreme measures

As membership of the European Union approaches for the front runners in the race to join the rich man's club, enthusiam is on the wane and nationalist politicians prey on popular fears

At the end of July, 47 Hungarian Roma arrived in Strasbourg to file a complaint with the European Court of Human Rights. They had been summarily evicted from their homes, which were destroyed after being declared unfit to live in, and relocated in appalling communal conditions. The families have applied for political asylum in France and are demanding compensation. Their campaign has been joined by about 250 Hungarian Roma in similar circumstances.

Hungary is the front runner in the competition for European accession, so all this comes as a bit of an embarrassment to the government. Particularly as in March, the Council of Europe's Commission against Racism and Intolerance noted that discrimination against Hungarian Roma remains a major problem. At about the same time government plans to distribute free contraceptives to Gypsies on the grounds that 'the increase of the Roma population is too great' were hastily withdrawn. It may have dawned on someone that parallels might be made with the notorious 1997 Czech policy of sterilising Gypsy women, sometimes without their knowledge. Yet in May, a new law was introduced giving the Hungarian authorities power to evict families without a court order and with no means of appeal. Two hundred people have been made homeless in recent weeks.

In the secure, impoverished, depressed world of communism where state and home were unconnected spheres, there was little concern about the broader social landscape. Today, public perception of what is acceptable or desirable for the community has changed little. Surveys suggest that 33% of Hungarians wouldn't allow Gypsy refugees into the country, and 47% approve of nightclubs where Roma are banned. European condemnation of racism is privately dismissed as hypocritical or meaningless. Much the same is true of EU directives on gay rights, transport, waste disposal or sausage. As far as most people are concerned, all Europe offers at the moment is admonishment.

'The EU is a kind of superego for this society,' says Peter György, chair of the media department at Budapest's leading university, ELTE. 'It's the controller, a metaphor for what we wanted to be. And a frustration. Everything we do is poor imitation. It's psychologically intolerable. What about our creativity? We feel like schoolchildren, or colonised peoples, unable to grow up. And sometimes, of course, depressed natures can rebel.'

As European integration assumes the shape of the inevitable and elites continue their obscure dialogue, little is being said in public about the darker side of accession. The only people prepared to address issues like unemployment, soaring prices and broken identity are political extremists. 'When you're not up to speed, untravelled, monolingual, and the new economic and social map seems unnavigable, nationalism is the cheapest, fastest way to defend your dignity,' György adds. 'The danger is that neo-Nazis will gain strength if mainstream parties don't find a realistic way of interpreting the situation.'

In Hungary, the far-right Justice and Life party (MIEP) helped the coalition government take over the boards that oversee state television and radio. Support for MIEP is expected to reach ten per cent by 2002. In Poland, where the ruling coalition is vulnerable to right-wing pressure, up to 20% of the population want to see a Haider-like figure on the political scene and 39% feel there is too much freedom. In the Czech Republic, the social democrat minority government is kept in power by the conservative, anti-European Civic Democratic Party (ODS). In Slovakia, the feisty populist leader, Vladimir Meciar, could be poised for a comeback.

Compromise and cooperation with extremists is a daily feature of central European parliamentary politics. Hungarian Prime Minister Viktor Orban's recent remark that 'there is life outside the EU' was interpreted by some as heralding a new coalition with the far right. The government is preparing for elections in 2002. Orban's aggressive push for a firm accession date is seen in Budapest as a tactic for appealing to Euro-pessimists at home, and even a way of provoking the EU into further delays. There are rumours of a new, right-wing political axis with Austria and Bavaria. 'The EU's 2002 deadline is our deadline too,' said deputy state secretary of the Hungarian foreign ministry Dénes Tomaj. 'If we are not accepted, the responsibility isn't ours. There's something wrong with the others.'

European sanctions against Austria and the EU's implicit ban on cooperation with the far right provoked a storm of defiance. Seventy-seven per cent of Hungarians supported the maintenance of diplomatic relations with Austria and Chancellor Wolfgang Schüssel's visit to Budapest in May. In a letter of solidarity to Schüssel, chairman of the Czech Chamber of Deputies and ODS leader Vaclav Klaus, said that Haider was 'a lesser evil than the attempt by the EU to speak out against the sovereign decision-making of one of its members'.

In July, the Polish weekly *Polityka* pointed out that now Austria's relations with its partners are on the mend, the country is finding a role for itself as a champion of Europe's smaller states. It is presenting itself as a voice for the inclusion of new, small members into the community, with similar rights and responsibilities, while at the same time fuelling the EU's anxieties about migration and security.

Fears of a massive cheap labour influx, and the EU's anxiety about losing its second line of defence along central Europe's eastern borders, threaten to cut across vital economic and political interests in the region. The Schengen treaty on border control will restrict long-established cultural and economic links, stunt the development of border regions, and are likely to create new tensions. At the moment, the Czech Republic and Slovakia have a free-trade agreement and workers cross the border freely. If the Czech Republic joins the EU early, its most open border will be closed. Hungary's links with its minorities in Romania with be similarly jeopardised, as will Estonian links with the other Baltic states. Poland's clampdown on the Ukrainian and Belarussian border two years ago provoked a storm of protest as communities in the east began to count the cost of lost 'suitcase trade' worth US$5 billion a year.

The cover of an August edition of the Polish weekly showed the photograph of a man netted by two masked border guards. The caption read: 'Frontier of the Worlds: half a million people wait to break through the eastern border.' The idea that the civilised world ends at the eastern frontier, wherever you happen to be, has underpinned government appeals to the EU and their own people for the past decade.

Dénes Tomaj talks about the need for Hungary to 'radiate its influence' into the less advanced countries on its borders. Lithuanian diplomats have referred to the return of Lithuania to its 'natural place in the international community' away from a 'Eurasian commonwealth ... foreign to most Lithuanians'.

The notion of the last frontier may be calculated to reinforce national identity and solidarity, and encourage public allegiance to the nation state and its political elite. If it promotes concern for stronger security and economic protection, it could be a useful tool for governments wanting to encourage a twofold allegiance: to the nation state and to a Europe that will facilitate the provision of development resources.

But as the western pledge to enlargement falters, public commitment to integration declines and the accession date slips, central European media are emphasising tensions between member states, bureaucratic inefficiency, indecision and delays. There is little analysis, and reports remain ostensibly pro-European, but the subtext reads that integration is a mask. The EU lacks political solidarity and common vision; it is fragmented and corrupt.

Central Europe is becoming more hardheaded about what integration may mean. Five years ago, people saw it more symbolically. In Romania or Bulgaria, where the prospect of accession is still dim, the EU enjoys 80% support. But in Poland, where the agricultural sector employs 20% of the population, people in the countryside are nervous about a squeeze that could reduce agricultural employment to a quarter of what it is now. Nationalists are suggesting that liberal reformers are so closely linked with Brussels that they may be incapable of negotiating effectively on Poland's behalf. A poll conducted in June 1999 showed that support for the EU had fallen to 54%. In 1996 it was 80%. Similar fears stalk Lithuania.

People are confused and everyone complains about inadequate information on the accession process, the European Commission, even local EU improvement programmes. 'The Polish authorities think of integration in technical terms, as something required by economic mechanisms,' said accession specialist Ireneusz Kaminski. 'But the mechanisms aren't transparent. People can't translate the technicalities into their own language.'

EU integration has always seemed to be a case of state formation at the level of elites and that's exactly how it's viewed in central Europe.

The rich man's club will go on talking to government elites while everyone else is told what's best for them.

'European identity came out of fear,' said Alexander Tomsky, director of Academia publishers in Prague. 'Two world wars persuaded people to integrate under the shadow of the nuclear threat. These pressures have gone. The Austrian situation is with us. It's hidden here, but it could surface ... And there's this thing of being told off all the time: you're not recycling enough, you don't look after your women ... A Czech referendum now would yield a 50:50 result.'

In July, the EU's Enlargement Commissioner, Gunter Verheugen, chastised candidate countries for involving the communist–era *nomenklatura* in their economies and politics, and for paying insufficient attention to the Copenhagen criteria (democracy, the rule of law, respect for human rights, a functioning market economy, and so on). But he has also acknowledged that if expansion fails to happen in the next six to ten years, candidates may be lost and countries destabilised.

As Europe tries to assuage its fear of movement, poverty and crime by 'socialising' the former communist states as cheaply as it can, it faces the fact that unless central eastern Europe develops consolidated liberal democracies, the western community's claim that its value system is universally applicable will weaken. And that could summon the spectre of a Europe bordered and riven by competing nationalisms, fallen alongside lost multinational federations like the former Soviet Union or Yugoslavia. ❏

Irena Maryniak

ROBERT WILLOUGHBY

China's evil genius

**Not since the Cultural Revolution have China's leaders
mobilised their forces so rabidly against an ideological enemy**

They didn't really radiate mystic menace, more the aura of
schoolchildren cadging fags behind the bike sheds. Our tai chi tutor
hustled us away this nippy Beijing morning, saying the furtive gang of
smokers, an odd clique of all ages and states of dress, huddled behind a
hedge, were a 'Special Chi Cong group'. 'Falun Gong,' say I. 'SHHH,'
demanded our lithe tutor. 'Yes, but quiet, you'll bring the police!'

This was the first time I'd seen these menaces to society, as I'd been
convinced they were in the course of a year's headlines in the *People's
Daily*, *China Daily*, the *People's Liberation* and other Xinhua (China News
Agency) outlets. It started with a bang on 22 July 1999:

'FALUN GONG DOOMED TO FAILURE'

'ANALYSIS OF FALUN GONG LEADER'S MALICIOUS
FALLACIES'

'TRUE FACE OF LI HONGZHI EXPOSED'

'FACTS PROVE LI HONGZHI, FOUNDER OF FALUN
GONG, IS AN EVIL FIGURE'

'CHINESE OFFICIAL DISMISSES FALUN GONG AS
RELIGION'

Scientists drew their own conclusions three days later:
'Chinese scientists are playing a major role in the nationwide
campaign to fight the notorious Falun Gong cult and create
greater public awareness about sciences in the country.'

And so it went on:
'LI HONGZHI MADE A FORTUNE OUT OF FALUN
GONG CLAIM EX-PRACTITIONERS.'

'FALUN GONG IS WELL ORGANISED: INSIDERS.
Key members of the outlawed Falun Gong sect say it has ulterior
political motives.'

'Currently, the nationwide campaign against the evil cult Falun
Gong has reaped a victorious struggle, yet the arduous and
complex tasks facing us have urged us to carry the battle through
to the end.' *People's Daily*, 23 July 2000

The ferocity and breadth of the campaign against the Falun Gong
expresses the fear felt by those in charge of China faced with what
could look like a rival for the affections of their people. The Falun Gong
is a 'pseudo-religion'; Li Hongzhi, its leader, a 'liar', 'heretic' and
'deceiver' in every media outlet open to the men in green; the religion
no more than 'foolishness based on fallacies ... a threat to the fabric of
society ... followers are misled ... responsible for the death of over 1,400
people ... non-scientific ... anti-religious ... a cult .... pure evil'.
But could it be that the Communist Party, for all the 'science' of its
beliefs used to destroy this flimsy 'cache of lies', has also fallen victim to
that most heartfelt, tortuous emotion, jealousy?

It's spent over 50 years persuading the people that communism was
the way to be. You didn't need any quasi-religious stuff, the only true
deities were Mao, Deng and Jiang, in the temple of Marx, with the red
book of truths. The enemies of poverty, foreign domination and worst,
division among the Chinese themselves, were defeated. It cost millions
dead, millions more exiled and the world shut out. In the terrible decade
of the Cultural Revolution, thousands of years of cultural thought were
wiped out in a stunning, desperate attempt to destroy any other ideas
except the truths of red, gold and rice. Now, they'd brought peace,
prosperity, new-found consumerism and, perhaps best of all, respect and
fear from previous rulers. Even earned the honour of having this century
designated 'China's century'. The sacrifices were huge, but so were the
gains.

Then Li Hongzhi turns up, sweeps five million off their feet, gives them that one element lacking in the staunchest of Partymen: spirituality. After all their achievements, all their efforts to persuade the people they didn't need these opiates, too many people, much too fast, proved that's exactly what they did want. Indeed, its followers are strong enough to defy the Party in public, sitting out on Tiananmen Square in these 'absurd' poses and getting carted off in paddy wagons, not brutally, since this is where the eyes of the world are watching, but with unfailing regularity.

They've given the world another stick with which to beat China. These ungrateful children of Mao are threatening to wreck everything. But they must be persuaded to see the error of their ways, not punished. Li Hongzhi must be proved to be a liar, heretic, deceiver, even a tax evader, a killer. Even in a society whose rules of the universe rest in science and man alone, he must become Satan incarnate.

Errant children don't take to this at all. Some do get killed when local frustration lashes out, but in the main they must be softly encouraged to make up their own minds, this cult is nothing but a cult. Anyone who renounces their FG vows is applauded, listened to, anyone continuing to believe these fallacies is 're-educated', 'adjusted' or, being beyond rescue, 'certified' for their own safety.

Perhaps the greatest irony in the end is not just that Falun Gong fills the 50-year-long vacuum, but that the Party drove away its own: 'Mental disorders hotbed for Falun Gong: expert' reads the headline. 'Stress, nervousness, anxiety and mental disorder have provided a hotbed for the Falun Gong cult in China,' says Wang Qingren, a professor with the Central University for Nationalities, in an exclusive interview with Xinhua on 27 July. 'Accustomed to cradle-to-grave employment, many people found it hard to adapt themselves quickly to the increased pressure and intensified competition of modern life,' Wang added. How did it all go so wrong? ❏

Robert Willoughby *is a freelance writer based in China*

The news fix

The economy is in a terrible state. There are factory workers who haven't been paid for months – because of mismanagement and corruption, as much as anything. Inflation is high enough to torment people on fixed incomes and, with unemployment already a major cause for concern, the country has to contend with the prospect of 800,000 people joining the job market each year in view of Iran's youthful population. But if you ask Iranians what they want, more often than not they'll tell you they want newspapers.

After President Khatami's election victory in 1997, a proliferating, colourful array of papers and journals began to weigh down the country's newspaper kiosks. Crowds thronged around them in the mornings to peruse the front pages and young boys wove between the cars at traffic lights, selling the favourite titles. In a country where the state has traditionally tended to ignore the people, these fresh, reformist newspapers, many of them run by Khatami's allies and associates, began to draw the people in and make them feel involved in, or at least aware of, the affairs of the nation.

They became the people's chosen representatives in circumstances in which the Majlis (parliament) and other state institutions were anything but representative. The papers made the people conscious of themselves and their own power. They convinced the readers of the importance of 'the fourth estate', as the seeing eye of the public and the nation's conscience: if brave journalists performed their task in exposing corrupt abusers of power, if they let their torches shine on the state's dark recesses and 'dark houses ', and if, at the same time, the people strengthened themselves by forming civil associations and made effective use of their votes in elections, the state could be turned into the servant of the people, rather than its cruel and indifferent master.

That, in a nutshell, was the reformist message. And people became acquainted with it not through Iranian radio and television, which is aggressively anti-Khatami. They learned about it by leafing through the pages of *Jameah* (Society), first published on 5 February 1998, banned on 23 July 1998, managing director: Hamid-Reza Jala'ipour; *Khordad* (the name of the month in which President Khatami was elected), first published on 3 December 1998, banned on 27 November 1999, managing director: Abdollah Nuri; *Sobh-e Emrooz* (This Morning), first published on 15 December 1998, banned on 27 April 2000, managing director: Sa'id Hajjarian; and *Mosharekat* (Participation), first published on 2 January 2000, banned on 27 April 2000, managing director:

Mohammad Reza Khatami, the president's brother; among others.

As Khatami's presidential term turned the halfway mark, journalists and ordinary people seemed to be falling into their new roles in the most exemplary fashion. In February 2000, the collaboration between the budding new 'fourth estate' and the increasingly confident nation reached new heights in the inspiring elections for the sixth term of the Majlis. The incoming Majlis deputies included many young faces, far fewer clerics and, not surprisingly, quite a few journalists.

Then came the backlash. Over 20 national reformist publication have died a death with 'temporary', pre-trial banning orders since the elections and it's almost impossible to keep track of the number of journalists now locked up in Tehran's Evin Prison: Mashallah Shamsolva'ezin (serving a two-and-a-half-year prison term since 10 April); Akbar Ganji (in prison since 22 April without trial); Emadeddin Baqi (sent to prison by the Press Court judge on 29 May before the end of his trial and subsequently sentenced to seven and a half years); Ahmad Zeidabadi (arrested at his home early on 7 August and detained since without charge; Massoud Behnoud (failed to return home after appearing before the Press Court judge for questioning on '85 charges' on 9 August and detained since); Ebrahim Nabavi (detained since 12 August on charges relating to 'slander and disseminating falsehood', based on his satirical columns); Mohammad Qouchani (detained since 13 August after appearing before the Press Court judge for questioning on unknown charges); are just some of the names in the endless roll-call of honour.

The nation's favourite journalists from the nation's favourite papers. All jailed, all banned. Khatami and the Majlis haven't been jailed and banned yet. But they've been told in no uncertain terms by the conservative faction that they must start solving the country's economic problems, and stop concerning themselves with 'peripheral issues'. And it's really true. The economy is in a terrible state. So what do the people want? Newspapers. ❏

Nilou Mobasser *is an Iranian writer and translator based in the UK*

A censorship chronicle incorporating information from the American Association for the Advancement of Science Human Rights Action Network (AAASHRAN), Amnesty International (AI), Article 19 (A19), Alliance of Independent Journalists (AJI), the BBC Monitoring Service Summary of World Broadcasts (SWB), the Committee to Protect Journalists (CPJ), Canadian Journalists for Free Expression (CJFE), Glasnost Defence Foundation (GDF), Instituto de Prensa y Sociedad (IPYS), The UN's Integrated Regional Information Network (IRIN), the Inter-American Press Association (IAPA), the International Federation of Journalists (IFJ/FIP), Human Rights Watch (HRW), the Media Institute of Southern Africa (MISA), Network for the Defence of Independent Media in Africa (NDIMA), International PEN (PEN), Open Media Research Institute (OMRI), Pacific Islands News Association (PINA), Radio Free Europe/Radio Liberty (RFE/RL), Reporters Sans Frontières (RSF), the World Association of Community Broadcasters (AMARC), World Association of Newspapers (WAN), the World Organisation Against Torture (OMCT) and other sources

ALGERIA

Nawal Ayadh, a journalist at the national television station, announced on 23 July that she was beginning a hunger strike in protest at her dismissal from ENTV. Ayadh was suspended in August 1998 after she became involved in a dispute with a senior police official at a press conference in the Ghardaia region. (IFJ)

ANGOLA

Voice of America (VOA) journalist

Isidoro Natalicio was evicted from his home on 20 June at the bidding of the attorney general. Natalicio, who rented the property from the government, was accused of 'diverse use of the residence': namely, using the house as an office. (MISA)

Twice on the night of 21 June, four soldiers raided the VOA's offices and attempted to gain access to the newsroom. The radio station's security guards were threatened at gunpoint, but refused to grant the men entry. (CPJ)

José Paulo, editor-in-chief of Catholic Radio Ecclesia, was kidnapped on 24 June by unknown assailants in Luanda. Paulo was being driven through the suburbs by his captors when their vehicle broke down, allowing him to escape through a hail of bullets. Ecclesia has fiercely criticised the government in recent months (*Index* 5/1999). (MISA)

The disruption to VOA operations continued on 20 July with the harassment of broadcaster **João de Almeida Domingos**. Domingos saw three men, including one in police uniform, breaking into his car, and later reported that work material, including computer disks and audio cassettes, had been stolen. (MISA)

Government officials harassed freelance journalist **Isaias Soares** throughout August. On 2 August authorities in the Malanje province placed an embargo on the broadcasting of his work after he reported on a sensitive military matter. On 7 August Soares was instructed to deliver his files and archives to the Office of Social

Communication for inspection and, on the subsequent day, he was effectively placed under house arrest when police officers were deployed outside his door. (MISA)

On 8 August writer **Rafael Marques** was denied permission to leave Angola to collect a prize bestowed on him by the Association of Black American Journalists. The restrictions are seen as an act of retribution by the government following the publication last July of a controversial article titled '*the Lipstick of Dictatorship*' (*Index* 1/00, 2/00, 3/00). (RSF)

ARGENTINA

TV journalist **Carlos Monsálvez** was threatened, beaten and mugged in separate incidents over a two-month period by unknown individuals allegedly acting on behalf of the provincial government of Neuquén. On 24 June Monsálvez, who is the Neuquén correspondent for TV news channel Todo Noticias, had his video camera stolen at gunpoint and his car vandalised and filled with garbage. Earlier, on 1 May, the reporter was beaten up in front of the provincial legislature. On 11 June, the occupants of a pick-up truck that drove up to him warned he would end up dead if he continued sending reports to Buenos Aires. (Periodistas)

Local dailies *La Voz del Interior* and *El Liberal* have been harassed with abusive flyers, threatening calls and phone tapping for criticising the government of the northern province of Santiago del Estero. The attacks started on 1 July when a van delivering copies of the

Córdoba-based *La Voz del Interior* was intercepted by an unregistered vehicle whose driver warned that future editions would be destroyed if the negative press coverage continued. On 1 August, the daily received an anonymous call warning that its correspondent in Santiago del Estero could end up in an 'accident'. Meanwhile, staffers of Santiago del Estero-based daily *El Liberal* began receiving threatening calls in mid-July and three of its journalists were insulted in flyers. The dailies criticised the authoritarian style of provincial governor Carlos Juárez and his wife, vice-governor Mercedes Aragonés. (Periodistas, CPJ)

A prominent banker linked to former president Carlos Menem made anti-Semitic remarks in a televised interview on 19 July against three journalists investigating fraud charges against him. Raúl Juan Pedro Moneta, who is suspected of irregularities in the liquidation of two banks, accused journalists **Horacio Verbitsky** (*Index* 6/1997, 6/1999), **Ernesto Tenembaum** and **Marcelo Zlotogwiazda** of picking on him as Jews for being a 'practising, devoted Catholic'. Moneta was indicted for the alleged fraud and spent six months on the run until the case against him was thrown out by the Federal Appeals Court. (Periodistas)

ARMENIA

On 8 July municipal authorities removed the newspaper *Azg* from news-stands in Gyumri because it contained an article critical of them. *Azg* said it planned to publish similar reports in the future. (Aragil Electronic News Bulletin)

AZERBAIJAN

On 3 July **Elkhan Hasanli**, a reporter with the independent daily *Yeni Musavat*, was covering the OSCE Minsk Group Briefing in Gazakh district when he was escorted from the proceedings by the chief of the district police acting on 'instructions from above'. (MPA News Agency)

The electricity supply to independent ANS TV station was cut off 15 minutes into the 14 July broadcast of an interview with Chechen rebel commander **Shamil Basayev**, who was shown describing the Azeri-Armenian conflict in Nagorno-Karabakh as 'a *jihad*'. Officials responsible for power supply claimed that the interruption was due to an accident. On 16 July ANS received an official notification, signed by Deputy Prosecutor-General Ramiz Rzayev, stating that the tape of the interview had been illegally imported from Russia and that the interview itself was illegal because it allegedly contained terrorist propaganda, in violation of international conventions ratified by Azerbaijan. Following another showing of the interview on 17 July, National Security Minister Namik Abasov phoned the editor-in-chief and threatened to shut down ANS if he attempted to broadcast the Basayev interview again. (CPJ, BBC)

Azadliq correspondent **Kebiran Dilaverli** was harassed by police as she covered a 17 July hunger strike by refugees from the Armenian-occupied Kelbajar district, who were demanding the release from prison of former interior minister Iskender Hamidov. (JuHI)

On 11 August **Khoshqedem Hidayetqizi**, editor-in-chief of the tri-weekly *Uch noqte*, received a court order from the Sabayil District Court of Baku City calling her to appear in court on 16 August. Attached was a letter from Minister of Press and Information Sirus Tebrizli, advising that a court ruling had already been issued against *Uch noqte* and, according to the new law on mass media, its publishing and distribution must be stopped. The new law came into effect on 13 February 2000, but the previous court ruling had been issued on 13 January 2000. (JuHI)

BANGLADESH

On 16 July **Shamsur Rahman**, a special correspondent with the Bengali national daily *Janakantha* and a regular contributor to BBC World Service radio, was shot dead by two unidentified men in his Jessore town office. No motive for the attack has come to light, but Rahman had in the past received death threats for his reportage from the smugglers and leftist groups that operate in the south-west of the country. (Media Watch, CPJ, RSF)

BELARUS

On 7 July ORT cameraman and Russian citizen **Dmitri Zavadski** disappeared at Minsk airport where he was due to meet one of ORT's station directors and friend **Pavel Cheremet** upon arrival of his flight. His car was found locked and parked outside the airport building. The two reporters had recently travelled to Chechnya to film a four-episode documentary called *The Chechen Diary*. Zavadsky's wife said that, shortly after they returned, her husband began to receive phone calls from an unknown man who insisted on a meeting. Zavadski left Belarussian state television to work for ORT in 1996 despite objections of President Alexandr Lukashenka, for whom Zavadsky had worked as personal cameraman. In July 1997 he was imprisoned along with Cheremt and sentenced to a suspended two-year prison term for violating the national border while preparing a documentary about smuggling between Belarus and Lithuania (*Index* 5/1997, 6/1997, 1/1998, 2/1998, 4/1998). (WAN, CPJ)

BOLIVIA

Freelance investigative journalist **Ronald Méndez Alpire** was shot at twice and injured in the leg by an unidentified assailant on 11 June in the city of Santa Cruz. Méndez was leaving the home of parliamentarian Roberto Landivar when the gunman shot him at close range and ran off. Landivar, who witnessed the attack, said the stranger seemed to deliberately shoot Méndez in the leg as a warning. The journalist has conducted numerous investigations into cases of corruption and drug trafficking. (IAPA, RSF)

BOSNIA-HERZEGOVINA

Muhammed Hamo Korda, who is affiliated with the ruling Party of Democratic Action (SDA), made a phone call on 11 July in front of witnesses in which he told **Edic Audic** of the Sarajevo-based weekly magazine *Slobodna Bosna* to prepare for a physical attack which took place an hour later. Korda was apparently angry about the magazine's coverage of alleged corruption associated with SDA-sponsored events. (RFE/RL)

BOTSWANA

Four journalists from the South African Broadcasting Corporation were detained on 20 June while filming the Dukwi Refugee camp for a special programme to mark Africa Refugee Day. Two correspondents were released immediately, but cameraman **Pat Pule** and reporter **Onene Chipuka**, who also writes for the *Voice*, were interrogated and instructed to seek permission before filming in future. (MISA)

BRAZIL

Reporter **Carina Paccola** of local daily *Folha de Londrina* had her pay suspended and was threatened with dismissal on 8 June by the owner, allegedly for defending seven colleagues fired the previous week. Paccola, who heads the Londrina branch of the National Federation of Journalists, questioned the redundancies, which were officially justified as a 'cost-cutting measure'. The daily's owner is former senator José Eduardo de Andrade Vieira. (IFJ)

Judge Adair Longhini in Río Branco has barred all press coverage of the upcoming municipal elections in the department of Acre, arguing that the coverage could be turned into 'propaganda'. (IFJ)

BRITAIN

Mohamed Al Fayed, the owner of Harrods, may face prosecution after permitting publication of an article written by renegade MI5 officer **David Shayler** in the September edition of his magazine *Punch* (*Index* 3/2000). Treasury officials claimed the article, allegedly disclosing the extent of the security service's ability to monitor IRA communications, would damage national security. A letter from government solicitors, alerting editor **James Sheen** to the consequences of allowing the piece to go to print, was also published. (*Press Gazette*)

On 2 August BBC governors reprimanded **John Humphrys**, the veteran radio broadcaster, for his treatment of Lord Robertson, the NATO secretary general, in an interview for Radio 4's *Today* programme about the Kosovo conflict. Humphrys was criticised for 'constantly interrupting' Lord Robertson and for 'snorting' as he tried to justify NATO's involvement in the war. The governors issued a strongly worded judgment stating Humphrys used the interview, broadcast during the run-up to the one-year anniversary of the NATO bombing campaign in February 1999, as a 'platform for his own opinions'. He has been told to adopt a different approach the next time the subject is covered. (*Guardian*)

Former MI5 officer **David Shayler** was arrested on his return to Britain on 21 August, and was charged with breaching the Official Secrets Act. Shayler fled to mainland europe in 1998 after publicly revealing MI5's mishandling of an investigation into IRA terrorist activity and alleging that MI6, the security agency for foreign affairs, had played an instrumental part in a

1996 plot to assassinate Libyan leader Colonel Moammar Qaddafi. Shayler maintains his innocence and plans to confirm in court the veracity of his allegations. On the same day, police dropped charges against student **Julie Ann Davies** who was arrested in March and accused of aiding and abetting Shayler (*Index* 3/2000). Davies had been a member of a group campaigning to have Shayler exonerated. (*Guardian, International Herald Tribune*)

BURMA

It was reported on 18 July that nine journalists for the banned monthly *Mojo*, which is linked to the opposition National League for Democracy, were arrested and jailed for collecting dissident news and distributing the magazine, which is published in Thailand. They face up to ten years, imprisonment. (Associated Press)

CAMBODIA

The Khmer and English-language *Cambodia News Bulletin* was suspended for 30 days, it was reported on 18 July, after re-publishing an article from the *South China Post* which called Prince Sihanouk 'mercurial' and 'capricious'. The government considered closing the paper permanently, the report continued, and refusing *Post* writer **William Barnes** admission to the country. (WAN)

CAMEROON

On 18 July **Daniel Atanga** and **Thierry Mbouza**, journalists with the bi-weekly *Dikalo*, were sentenced to six months in prison by a Yaoundé Court of First Instance. Editor **Celestin Biake Difana** also received a six-month suspended sentence. The three were accused of publishing a memorandum in November 1998, signed by 81 road hauliers, which described their union as 'a phantom structure, led by one Pierre Sime, which helps expatriate hauliers plunder Cameroon'. (RSF).

CENTRAL AFRICAN REPUBLIC

Maka Gbossokotto, director of the privately owned daily *Le Citoyen*, was summoned to Bangui police headquarters on 4 August after a complaint by Prosper N'Douba, communications adviser to President Ange-Felix Patassé. N'Douba had written to a number of private companies offering for sale 'new official portraits of the president'. Gbossokotto published the contents of N'Douba's letter under the headline, 'Companies racket organised by Prosper N'Douba?' He is now charged with defamation. (WAN).

CHINA

Falun Gong adherents continue to fall foul of the authorities in numbers too great to record here in detail. For fully referenced information about victims of the persecution from 7 June to 7 August, please visit: www.indexoncensorship.org/news

Zhang Hongbao, the fugitive founder and leader of another outlawed group, Zhong Gong (*Index* 2/2000 3/2000 4/2000, and his assistant **Yan Qinxing**, were granted political asylum by Hawaiian authorities on 16 June. The decision on his asylum was subsequently suspended following demands from the Chinese embassy in Washington that he be extradited. On 8 August, the Hong Kong-based Information Centre of Human Rights and Democratic Movements in China, claimed 100,000 people had lost their jobs with the closure last July of 3,000 enterprises connected to Zhong Gong. A further 600 people are said to be in police detention without any visitation rights. (Agence France-Presse, Associated Press, Information Centre of Human Rights and Democratic Movements in China)

Journalist and economist **He Qinglian** was removed from her post as senior editor of the *Shenzhen Legal Daily* on 21 June at the behest of government officials. Her demotion to researcher within the paper followed publication in *Shuwu* magazine of an article in which she used official figures to describe China's 'highly abnormal social structure' where 'One per cent of the population controls 60% of the wealth'. Chinese media have been ordered not to reproduce any of her work and *Shuwu* was threatened with closure. In a recent interview, Ms He said: 'I am not afraid to face the consequences of saying that China now has the most depraved group of governing elites in the last 1,000 years of Chinese history.' (*International Herald Tribune*, RSF, WAN)

Plans to publish *Waiting*, a novel by US resident **Ha Jin**, have been cancelled by a publishing house in China, it was reported on 22 June. The novel, which has won two prestigious prizes in the US, is the story of a military doctor trying over many years to extricate himself from an arranged marriage so he can marry the nurse he loves. (Associated Press)

On 7 July police raided a gym in Guangzhou, arresting 37 gay men on charges of prostitution under a 1993 directive which states homosexual activity 'twists sexuality, runs counter to public morality, destroys the social atmosphere [and] wrecks family harmony'. (Agence France-Presse, Associated Press)

Fears about academic freedom in post-handover Hong Kong have arisen following claims by Dr **Robert Chung** of Hong Kong University (HKU) that he was warned to stop conducting opinion polls on the popularity of Beijing-appointed Chief Executive Tung Chee-hwa. Dr Chung alleged on 7 July in the *South China Morning Post* that 'More than once, I was given a clear message from Tung via a special channel that my polling activities were not welcome [...] Tung did not like me polling his popularity or the government's credibility.' Tung's office have denied the allegations, as has the 'special channel' mentioned by Dr Chung – HKU's vice-chancellor, Prof **Cheng Yiu-chung**. (Hong Kong iMail, Reuters, *South China Morning Post*)

A state-run television station in Zhuhai, near Macau, fired the chief of its news department, **Lin Shufu**, and reprimanded several senior journalists and staff following a report on 9 July covering the opening of a cable TV station in Macau. During the

report TV cameras inadvertently focused on monitors in the Macau studios which happened to be showing a two-second clip of students confronting tanks during the 1989 demonstrations on Tiananmen Square. (Associated Press)

Minister of Culture Sun Jiazhen announced on 11 July that Beijing is to step up 'positive education' on the Internet to combat portals deemed guilty of posting 'pornographic, reactionary, violent and deceitful' content. It was confirmed on 15 July that **Huang Qi**, who ran a site carrying articles about the Tiananmen Square massacre of 1989 (*Index 4/2000*) is to face charges of subversion. On 16 July **Zhang Weiying**, deputy director of the Guanghua Management Institute at Beijing University, lambasted the government's over-regulation of the Internet and IT industries. 'When a new technology appears in China, the first reaction of our government is to try to find a way to regulate it [...] What the economy needs is actually a free environment,' he said in a speech published by the *Security Times* newspaper. The official news agency Xinhua announced on 5 August that at least 20 provinces and cities are to set up special Internet police to 'administer and maintain order' on the Internet. It reported that one such unit in Anhui Province has already tried cases of 'cheating, property embezzlement and pornography.' *A People's Daily* commentary on 9 August claimed the Internet has made 'political thought work' more efficient, but had also brought 'unwelcome ideas.' It repeated warnings of 'foreign

enemies' using the Internet 'to infiltrate us'. An enormous publicity campaign was announced on 10 August by the Communist Party's Publicity Department to enhance the status of nine official websites carrying online news. Other news organisations are banned from publishing 'positive reports' about sites not among the 'Big Nine', which are all branches of existing official print and broadcast outlets.' (Agence France-Presse, Associated Press, ChinaOnline.com, Hong Kong iMail, Human Rights in China, Reuters, *South China Morning Post*)

News emerged on 17 July of the 13-year prison sentence handed down to **Gao Qinrong**, a journalist from official Xinhua news agency. He filed a report in 1998 exposing widespread corruption and incompetence surrounding a multi million-dollar irrigation project in Shanxi Province. The story was widely picked up by the national media eager to answer recent calls from the national leadership to expose corruption. Outraged officials responsible for the failure of the irrigation project ordered Gao's arrest and arranged charges of embezzlement, bribery and pimping. He was sentenced to 13 years following a closed one-day trial on 29 April 1999. No officials from Shanxi have been held to account. (Agence France-Presse, Associated Press, CPJ, *South China Morning Post*)

It was reported on 23 July that *Devils on the Doorstep*, the latest film by **Jiang Wen** and winner of the Grand Prix Jury Prize at Cannes this year, has been banned by the Film Censorship Committee of the

XIN WEMING
New Culture clubbed

On August 3 the Ministry of State Security shut down New Culture Forum, China's first pro-democracy website. The ministry also brought calamity on our Internet Service Provider (ISP), the Beijing-based Million Internet Company, paralysing its business. We severely protest against the ministry's suppression of the human right to freedom of expression. We express our deep apologies to the Million Internet Company and its general manager, and we offer our sincere gratitude to the people from all walks of life who have visited our site and shown concern for New Culture Forum.

Humanity has entered the age of Internet information. People use it to exchange ideas and to transmit messages. It is a historic trend that cannot be blocked or reversed. Human rights, democracy and the rule of law are values of most people in the world today. Respect for opposition factions, the protection of minorities and individual freedoms are political principles followed by present-day civilised society. A normal, civilised government must tolerate different voices and accept scrutiny and criticism. Only then can the government remain honest and secure the cooperation of its tax-paying people. No system or government is perfect; they all must constantly adapt, change and improve, based upon the wishes of the people. All rulers need to be monitored and face constructive criticism. It is based on this belief that we established the New Culture Forum website.

On the one hand, the government claims to represent advanced productive forces but, on the other, it wantonly censors the Internet by shutting down websites. In the age of Internet information, the Chinese government continues with the mindset of clamping down and violating freedom of expression in the hope of maintaining autocratic, totalitarian rule. This is not just a problem of the present; it will cause disaster in the future. ❏

Xin Weming (meaning New Culture), hosted by a Beijing ISP but run from Shandong Province, was shut down on 3 August by officials who said it was 'too sharp' and 'too anti-government'. Those running the site have since gone into hiding, but they issued this statement on 12 August. Under new regulations, Li Tao, the ISP's owner, could face penalties for failing to control its content.

State Administration of Radio, Film and Television. The film is a tragi-comedy about villagers capturing and collaborating with Japanese soldiers during the Anti-Japanese War (1937–45). What purports to be the committee's report on his work has circulated on the Internet since May. It states the film 'severely distorts history' and 'The behaviour of the Chinese civilians depicts the Chinese as not hating the Japanese troops as they should [...] The Chinese are depicted as extremely ignorant and unable to recognise their enemy.' Jiang might be ordered to surrender the negative of the film and could possibly be banned from acting or directing in China for seven years. (Agence France-Presse, Associated Press, Asia E!Online.)

The poet and long-time US resident, **Bei Ling**, was arrested in Beijing on 11 August on unknown charges. Hundreds of copies of *Tendency*, a literary journal privately published by Bei, were confiscated from a bar near Beijing University. The journal, which featured work by Seamus Heaney and photographs of Chinese dissidents, has previously been accused by Beijing of having 'political problems'. (Associated Press.)

Ma Xiaoming, a journalist with Shanxi TV (*Index* 4/1998), was detained by police on 12 August having ignored official warnings and spoken with an anonymous US journalist about farmer unrest in the region. (Associated Press, Reuters.)

COLOMBIA

Lawyer and journalist **Eduardo Pilonieta** survived an assassination attempt on 14 June after being shot at three times by two unknown assailants on motorbikes. Pilonieta, a regular contributor to the daily *Vanguardia Liberal* in Bucaramanga, is in a stable condition. (RSF, WAN)

Members of the leading guerrilla group FARC grabbed and burned 3,000 copies of daily *El Tiempo* on 20 June. Two other deliveries were attacked in April by FARC and the National Liberation Army (ELN). The FARC is believed to have been behind the assassination attempt against the daily's editor, **Francisco Santos Calderón**, now hiding in Miami. (CPJ)

Marisol Revelo Barón became the fourth journalist to be murdered this year after an unidentified gunman shot her on 4 July at home in the Pacific town of Tumaco. Revelo worked as the information officer of a local state-run environmental agency, Corponariño. Before that, she was news editor of local radio station Radio Mira and a reporter for TV channels Teletumaco and Impacto Televisión. The 25-year-old died instantly after being hit by three bullets in the stomach. (CPJ, IPI, IFJ, IAPA)

COTE D'IVOIRE

On June 23 Information Minister Captain Cesar Sama announced that the ruling CNSP would soon release measures designed to curtail the publication of any information likely to negatively affect the credibility of journalists, national security and social peace. Captain Sama who replaced journalist **Levy Niamkey** as information minister on 19 May, accused local newspapers of being 'opposition mouthpieces' and said that he 'would not hesitate to make use of laws which provide a spate of punishments for journalists who deliberately ... compromise national security' through their reporting. (RSF)

On 5 July the offices of private radio Nostalgie FM were officially shut down. No official reasons were given but the ruling junta is thought to have been reacting against a 4 July programme that allowed a soldiers' representative to air a protest over the non-payment of a US$9,000 bonus to each soldier who participated in the successful coup of 24 December 1999 by General Robert Guei. On the same day, ten heavily armed soldiers searched the premises of Nostalgie after which personnel were dismissed and the station's keys were confiscated. (RSF)

On 6 July **Sy Savane** and **Hien Solo**, respectively publisher and editor-in-chief of the state-operated daily *Fraternité-Matin*, were sacked by presidential decree for their alleged pro-opposition postures. Another decree on the same day terminated the employment of **Kone Lancine** and **Traore Abou**, editor-in-chief and news director respectively, with the state-owned television network RTI. (RSF)

Le Libéral was ordered closed on 7 July for an indefinite period as a result of the paper's perceived affiliation with the Rasseublement des Républicains (RDR) and a front-page article headlined, '12,000 mutineers want CFA78b'. The report charged that General Geui's military regime was at the mercy of the 12,000-strong army. (RSF).

Yves Zogbo, vice-director of Nostalgie FM, and five print journalists were summoned to the offices of General Guei on 6 July for questioning in connection with an alleged military mutiny. The two papers and the radio station involved are allegedly aligned with the opposition RDR. The junta suspects RDR leader Allassane Outtarra of precipitating the unrest that swept the country on 4 July, claiming the lives of three soldiers and one civilian. The summoned journalists were publisher **Kone Yoro**, photographer **Tano Emmanuel** and office manager **Diomandee Ibrahim**, from *Le Libéral*; and publisher **Patrice Guehi** and editor-in-chief **Meite Sindou** of *Le Patriote*. Editor-in-chief **Sran Haizy** of the private daily *Le Jeune Démocrate* was briefly detained and interrogated in a military base near Abidjan on 6 July. All were released after they were forced to crawl, sing pro-junta anthems and perform 150 push-ups. (RTF)

Military ruler General Guei sent a grim message to local journalists warning them of a systematic crackdown in the aftermath of what he described as a 'failed coup'. Guei told a press conference on 7 July that 'from now on, bias and distortion of facts by the press will be systematically punished'. He alleged that the ruling National Public Salvation Committee had collected 'evidence' that local journalists had received payments from political parties in exchange for writing negative stories about the military regime. (RSF)

On 31 July **Mohamed Fofana Dara**, a journalist with the Abidjan bureau of the BBC's Africa Service, was beaten by two soldiers while covering a demonstration close to the French embassy. The protesters were demonstrating support for statements made by France's Minister for Development Charles Josselin concerning the country's electoral process. (RSF).

Yore Kone and **Khristain Kera**, managing editor and journalist respectively of *Le Libéral*, were held for questioning on 2 August at Abidjan police in connection with a slander inquiry initiated by General Guei. The article by Kera, entitled 'Guei personally signs a cheque for CFA850m to finance his future election campaign', follows the 7 July posting of information on the Africa Intelligence website, accusing Guei of managing funds whose origins are unknown. (RSF)

RSF correspondent **Ricardo González Alfonso** was detained on 15 July by officials from the State Security Department and subjected to a six-hour interrogation, before being released. No explanation was offered. (RSF)

Two independent journalists from the Santiago Press agency were viciously assaulted by police while covering a rally marking the anniversary of the sinking of a civilian ship. **Marilyn Lahera** and **José Antonio** were beaten by officers at the mid-July march, where protesters demanded an investigation into the torpedoing of the *13 de Marzo* by armed forces six years ago. (IAPA)

Patric Musuyi Mugala, journalist with the public radio station RTNC, and **Jérôme Ngandu Muyembe**, director of television information with the same network, were dismissed and indefinitely suspended by director José Kajangwa, it was reported on 19 June. The two journalists were accused of having broadcast the opinions of the FECODI (Congolese Diamond Federation) members concerning a scandal in which a 267-carat diamond belonging to a private citizen was seized by the government. The FECONDI views were broadcast on both public and radio and television stations in late June. The case was both front page news in both local and international media. (Journaliste en Danger)

Polydor Muboyayi Mubanga, publisher of the daily *La Phare*, was summoned to the Council of State Security and interrogated over an unsigned article in the 19 June edition, entitled 'Kazadi Nyembe: the masks are starting to come off'. The article called for an end to end the 'tribalisation' of a commission appointed to hear ministers and managing directors on their administrations. Mubanga was accused of 'inciting tribal hatred'. (Journaliste en Danger)

Publisher of the weekly *Le Carousel* **Aimé Kakese Vinalu** was arrested on 23 June and charged with 'threatening state security'. He was to appear before the Court of Military Order over publication of two articles in the 22 June edition, entitled 'Kabila-Victor Mpoyo dispute' and 'A call for opposition unity'. The prosecution claimed that the purpose of the editorial was to 'incite the Congolese opposition to rebel against the established power'. Kaseke said he had been severely beaten in detention. (WAN)

Managing Editor **Bonane Yangazi** of *Vision* newspaper was arrested and its offices ransacked on 10 July by officers of the National Information Agency (NIA) officers who also seized the paper's computers, archives and a radio. Yangazi had recently been elected to parliament. The NIA commanding officer said, 'Tell your colleagues not to tell stupidities about this matter. Otherwise, they'll have to deal with me.' (WAN)

Journalist **Crepin Casino Mbeto** of *Le Choc* was arrested on 15 July at his home in Quesso for reporting on confrontations with police at the local airfield. (RSF)

BBC television producer **Caroline Parr** was detained in Kinshasa by the security services on 26 July, along with her assistant **Pierre Mombele** and **Jonas Munkamba**, whom she was interviewing about the 1961 assassination of Patrice Lumumba. (*Daily Telegraph*)

DOMINICAN REPUBLIC

Journalists celebrated a victory for free speech in the country on 7 August, following the conviction of four army officers for the murder in 1975 of *Ahora* editor **Orlando Martínez**, a critic of the government. (IAPA)

EGYPT

University professor **Saad El Din Ibrahim** was arrested on 30 June and charged with a variety of offences, including the dissemination of 'provocative propaganda'. Ibrahim, a director of the non-governmental organisation (NGO) Ibn Khaldoun Centre for Development, was apprehended along with four colleagues from the institution while working on a project designed to monitor the fairness of the forthcoming parliamentary elections. Documents from the Ibn Khaldoun Centre were seized by security police, who later shut down the social science faculty in which Ibrahim worked. (A19, Egyptian Organisation for Human Rights)

The government's crackdown on NGOs continued with the forcible closure of the Hay'at Da'am al-Nakhibat group on 5 July. The organisation, which encourages women to participate in elections, was accused of intent to damage the country's 'international reputation'. (HRW)

Journalists at the recently defunct *Al Shahab* (*Index* 3/1998, 4/1998, 5/1998, 6/1998, 5/1999, 3/2000, 4/2000) called off their hunger strike on 20 July when the government agreed to pay their salaries until the newspaper's fate is decided. On the same day, however, theology professor **Yehia Ismail Hablush** was charged with insulting and defaming Mohammed Sayyed Tantawi, the grand sheikh of Al Azhar University, in an article published in a 1999 edition of *Al Shahab*. (*Cairo Times*)

Prosecutors announced on 22 July that **Mohamed Al Gheiti**, a writer at *Al Meydan* newspaper, would stand trial for insulting Ahmed Omar Hashem, a director of Al Azhar University. Gheiti criticised Hashem in an article published in the independent paper for guiding the university 'from bad to worse'. (*Cairo Times*)

The Egyptian Organisation for Human Rights (EOHR) registered its alarm on 31 July after the government refused to grant the movement NGO status (*Index* 3/2000). The organisation alleges that the Ministry for Social Affairs reneged on its earlier pledge to allow EOHR to be registered as an NGO as part of its escalating war on independent movements. Under a law passed in June 1999 (*Index* 4/1999, 5/1999), any NGO not officially sanctioned is effectively barred from functioning. (A19, Egyptian Organisation for Human Rights)

EQUATORIAL GUINEA

Fearing imprisonment after a warrant for his arrest was issued, journalist **Alphadio Modesto Ayibatin** fled the country on 25 June. Two days earlier, the state prosecutor's office had demanded that Ayibatin be put on trial for 'discrediting and defaming the government' after an article critical of President Teodoro Mbasogo's economic policy was printed in Canada's daily *Le Droit*. (CPJ, AI)

AMIR EDDIN IBRAHIM
My father

My father Dr Saad Eddin Ibrahim, a political sociology professor at American University, Cairo, was arrested at gun point in our house in Maadi during the late hours of 30 June. Over 35 armed state security guards raided our home and confiscated our personal computer, our family safe and many of my dad's personal papers. Fortunately, the family did not witness this scene.

My father was initially detained for 15 days while investigations were conducted. He was charged with harming Egypt's reputation, voter registration fraud, international bribery and receiving foreign funds without government permission. I will not go into the details of these accusations, other than to say that anyone who has ever taken a class, knows or has worked with my father can attest to how honest he is. He strongly believes in transparency. The Ibn Khaldun Research Centre, the focus of the controversy, was the first Egyptian NGO to publicly disclose all its projects and sources of funding on the Internet. It has been legally registered since 1988, consistently paying all its taxes on an annual basis and complying with all domestic laws.

On 13 July, the state prosecutor extended my father's detention for another 15 days. They have searched the Ibn Khaldun Research Centre three times, and raided an independent sister NGO, Support Centre for Women Voters, in the hope of finding something incriminating. Meanwhile, the national press has waged an all-out character assassination of him. Luckily, the international media has dealt with this story objectively, but for the most part public opinion has been led to believe that my dad is a western agent, a spy and a traitor.

My father's intentions of repeating what he had done in 1995, by forming an independent monitoring and observation team to assess the fairness of the upcoming parliamentary elections in November, did not fit the state's agenda. But, one week after his detention, the Supreme Court validated his 1995 conclusions and declared the entire People's Assembly unconstitutional!

My father is being used to set an example to the rest of Egypt's intellectuals. It is a clear attempt to terrorise the voice of independent and progressive forces in our country. ❏

FIJI

Several media professionals were either detained or wounded during the abortive coup attempt by George Speight and his followers (*Index* 4/2000). On 27 May **Jerry Harmer**, a cameraman for Associated Press, was shot while filming a confrontation between about 150 coup supporters and a dozen government troops. On 28 June, ten foreign and six local journalists from the *Fiji Times*, *Fiji Sun*, Fiji TV, FM96, *Sydney Morning Herald*, Reuters TV, Australia Broadcasting Corporation and Radio New Zealand were detained for two hours after a press conference. On 4 July, **Sitiveno Moce**, a photo-journalist with the *Fiji Sun*, was also detained at a press conference, interrogated and threatened. As he was leaving parliament he was badly beaten and robbed of his camera equipment and personal possessions. (Pacific Islands News Association)

FRANCE

On 17 July the Council of State ruled that websites could not be promoted via television (Internet Age)

On 11 August Judge Jean-Jacques Gomez confirmed his 22 May judgment that Internet portal Yahoo must abide by French law even overseas, and therefore either remove pages related to Nazi memorabilia from its US website, or block French citizens from accessing the site. The judge set a further hearing for 6 November to discuss technical means of complying with his ruling.

GAMBIA

On 20 June **Madi Cessay**, editor of *Gambia News and Report* magazine, was charged along with 25 members of the opposition United Democratic Party (UDP) with the murder of Alieu Njai, a driver with the ruling AFRC. On 18 June Madi and about 100 UDP members, including the party leader Ousainou Darbo, were detained at a police station in Basse, about 400 kilometres from Banjul. They were taken there after the UDP campaign party ran into an ambush by the supporters of the ruling party in which Njai died. The detainees were denied access to anyone, including relatives. (IFJ). On 10 August the offices of independent Radio 1FM were attacked by ten unidentified persons who sprayed tear gas on the proprietor and two staff members, who suffered serious injuries. (West African Journalists Association)

Alhaji Yorro Jallow and **Bada Galleh Jallow**, managing editor and editor-in-chief respectively of the private Banjul daily *Independent*, were interrogated by immigration officials who questioned their citizenship. The Jallows' aged parents were also subjected to questioning. The editors believe the sessions were in reprisal for a 19 June article which reported that an elected chief had been sacked, and a ruling party official was appointed as his replacement. (CPJ)

GEORGIA

On the night of 24 July, **Vasil Silagadze**, a reporter with independent daily *Eko Digest*, was stopped in his car by two plain-clothes police officers checking identification papers. They recognised him as the author of an article, entitled 'Police officers live very well without salaries', which had appeared in *Eko Digest* on 18 June. The article condemned high-ranking police officials, including the interior minister, for their 'luxurious lifestyle' while low-ranking officers were poorly paid and often wait months for their salaries. The officers demanded Silagadze disclose his sources for the article, and, when he refused, they beat him severely and slashed the fingers of his right hand. They threatened further abuse if he persisted in covering the issue of police corruption. (WAN, RSF, RFE/RL, CPJ)

GERMANY

The government of ex-chancellor Helmut Kohl destroyed millions of key documents in a carefully planned operation after it lost the 1998 general election, a special investigation announced on 28 June. The discovery adds a new dimension to the parliamentary inquiry into a scandal over illegal donations to Kohl's Christian Democratic Union. (*Daily Telegraph*)

GUATEMALA

The news agency Centre of Informative Reports on Guatemala has received a series of threats from unknown sources. On 23 June, an anonymous caller promised to 'kill' members of the organisation while, on 10 July, director **Ilmeana Alamilla** was told to 'watch herself'. The news agency is linked with the Guatemalan National Revolutionary Unity party, an opposition movement. (RSF)

Simon Davies on

PRIVACY

Ursula Owen on

HATE SPEECH

Patricia Williams on

RACE

Gabriel Garcia Marquez on

JOURNALISM

John Naughton on

THE INTERNET

...all in INDEX

GUINEA

The press regulatory body, the CNC, ordered on 28 July that the press accreditations of Agence France-Presse correspondent **Mouctar Bah**, **Ben Douda Sylla** of Africa 1 and the BBC's **Amadou Dialla** be withdrawn for two months. The three were accused of pursuing a 'hidden agenda' and reporting 'tendentious and malevolent information on Guinea's socio-political situation'. (CPJ, RSF)

INDIA

Recent anti-Christian violence in Uttar Pradesh State continued in the first week of June, when Catholic priest **George Kunjhikandam** was beaten to death in Mathura. That same week, two bombs exploded outside churches in the southern state of Andhra Pradesh, another exploded outside a church in neighboring Karnataka and a fourth was detonated outside a church in Goa. (*Guardian*)

Parag Saikia, a journalist with the daily *Aji*, was beaten on 6 July by LN Tamuly, a magistrate in the town of Sibsagar in Assam. Saikia had been summoned by Tamuly and reproached for publishing an article on 1 July about the local authorities' alleged involvement in corruption. (RSF)

V Selvaraj, a correspondent for the bi-weekly newspaper *Nakkeeran* in Perambalur, Tamil Nadu, was shot dead on 31 July. Eight suspects were arrested by police within an hour of the murder, but no motive has come to light. (RSF)

On 10 August **Pradeep Bhatia**, a photo-journalist with the daily *Hindustan Times*, was killed in a bomb blast in Srinagar, the summer capital of Jammu and Kashmir. Nine other journalists were injured in the bombing, for which the separatist *Hizbul Mujahidin* claimed responsibilty. (RSF, CPJ)

The same day 20 employees of the local department of information in Calcutta attacked several journalists while they were covering an event inside the administration building. The civil servants, members of a union affiliated to the Communist Party of India-Marxist (CPI-M), criticised the journalists for 'supporting' the representatives of another labour union. On 13 August several journalists were attacked by CPI-M Supporters during the municipal elections in Barrackpore, West Bengal State. (RSF)

Recent Publications: *The Prevention of Terrorism Bill 2000. Past Abuses revisited?* (AI, June 2000, pp 15); *A trail of unlawful killings in Jammu and Kashmir: Chithisinghpora and its aftermath* (AI, June 2000, pp 14)

INDONESIA

The editorial staff of the *Siwa Lima*, published in Ambon, capital of the Moluccas, received death threats on 23 June from an officer of the Islamist militia, Laskar Jihad. The journalists went into hiding for two days. Laskar Jihad has allegedly brought thousands of volunteers to the islands to take part in the 'holy war' against Christians which has claimed 4,000 lives since January 1999. (RSF)

Edi Saputra Hasibuan, a reporter from *Pos Kota*, was attacked by members of the Islamic Defender Front as he covered the group's protest in front of the National Police Headquarters in South Jakarta on 7 July. He was attacked for allegedly defaming the group's operational division deputy chairman, Alwi Usman. (AJI)

On 29 July **Ahmad Ibrahim**, a *Serambi* journalist, was attacked by a Mobile Brigade officer in a café in Lhoksukon, Northern Aceh District where he planned to report on 5,000 returning refugees. (AJI)

IRAN

On 25 June a Tehran religious court ordered the indefinite closure of reformist daily newspaper *Bayan*, edited by **Hojatoleslam Ali-Akbar Mohtashemi**, a close adviser to President Mohammed Khatami. *Bayan*, which was launched in December 1999, had 'broken the laws of Islam'. (RSF)

There is mounting concern over the safety of journalist **Ezzatollah Sahabi** and translator **Khalil Rostamkhani**, who were detained following their participation in a Berlin conference held in April (*Index* 4/2000). Sahabi, managing editor of the daily *Iran-e-Farda* ('Iran Tomorrow'), was reportedly arrested on 26 June, following intense questioning at Branch 3 of the Revolutionary Court in Tehran. Rostamkhani, apparently arrested for translating at the same event, is being held in incommunicado detention. (Writers in Prison Committee).

On 18 July Tehran's press court sentenced journalist **Emadeddin Baqhi** of the daily *Fatth* to five and a half years' imprisonment for publishing articles 'in breach of Islamic Law' (*Index* 4/2000). He wrote extensively about the unexplained murders of intellectuals and dissidents in 1998 (*Index* 1/1999). (MENA)

On 25 July, the press court ordered the closure of the reformist weekly *Goonagoon,* four weeks after it first hit the news-stands. Editor-in-chief **Fatmeh Farahmandpour** was summoned to court a day earlier for 'insulting government officials'. *Goonagoon* is the twentieth newspaper since April to be shut down. (RSF)

On 1 August **Taqi Rahmani**, journalist for the banned reformist daily newspaper *Iran-e-Farda*, and **Mohammed Reza Zohdi**, head of the outlawed reformist daily *Arya*, were both sentenced to four months' imprisonment. Zohdi was subsequently banned from taking part in any press activities on the grounds that he was 'spreading lies' and 'violating the election of law'. (RSF)]

On 2 August Tehran's Press Court ordered the closure of the reformist daily *Bahar*, following publication of an article in which **Mohammed-Reza Khatami** is said to have criticised Ayatollah Khameni's decision to withdraw 'from the parliament's agenda an amendment to the press law that was to liberalise journalism' as 'a plot organised against parliament'. (RSF, *International Herald Tribune*)

As the crackdown on the independent press strengthened, the Press Court on 7 August ordered the arrest of pro-reform journalist **Ahmad Zeidabadi**.

Abadi works for *Hamshahri*, Iran's largest pro-reformist newspaper. (*International Herald Tribune*)

Journalist and researcher **Hojjatoleslam Hassan Youssefi Eshkevari** was arrested on 5 August in Tehran for his part in the Berlin conference in April (*Index* 4/2000). His detention comes as a direct response to a speech Eshkevari gave which was deemed by the Special Court for the Clergy as 'a campaign against the system … denying and insulting the holy religion of Islam'. Eshkevari was once a contributing editor at the banned daily *Iran-e-Farda*. (AI)

On 9 August the justice ministry issued a warrant of arrest for the journalist **Massoud Behnoud**, close to the reformists. He is supposed to answer for 85 complaints lodged against him, some of them by the fundamentalist group Ansar-Hezbollah. A pre-revolutionary TV reporter, Behnoud has refused to appear in court. After 10 years of 'professional silence', Massoud Behnoud took a stand in favour of President Khatami in the presidential elections of 1997. Since then he has collaborated with several now banned newspapers and frequently spoken on foreign radio stations in Persian. (RSF)

Journalists **Ebrahim Nabavi** and **Mohammad Ghoutchani**, both with *Asr-e-Azadegan*, were arrested on 12 and 13 August respectively. Nabavi, who underwent intensive interrogation before the Press Court, is well known for his satirical articles. (RSF)

JORDAN

The Jordanian Press Association decided on 3 August to take disciplinary action against its own Secretary-General, **Nidal Mansour**, for his 'liaison' with the non-governmental organisation, the Centre for Defending Freedom of Journalists. Mansour had been trying to encourage the right to freedom of speech for journalists. (A19)

KAZAKHSTAN

On 6 July the state-owned company Dauir refused to continue printing the Russian/English-language bi-weekly *Vremya Po*, on the grounds that the paper had an overdue balance. Local sources said the real reason was that officials had pressured Dauir to stop printing *Vremya Po* after its 3 July edition reprinted articles on a corruption scandal implicating President Nursultan Nazarbayev that had already appeared in *Newsweek* and the *Wall Street Journal*. Since 6 July, the paper has only been able to publish on the Internet. (CPJ)

On 17 July *SolDat* editor-in-chief **Yermurat Bapi** and director **Argyngazy Madiyanov** were charged with criminal defamation against President Nursultan Nazarbayev for reprinting articles from the websites of the US magazine *Fortune* and the Italian newspaper *Corriera della Sera* about alleged corruption in the government. The stories in the weekly newspaper alleged that top officials, including Nazarbayev, had accepted massive bribes from US and Russian businessmen in exchange for favourable contracts to reprocess iron and aluminium ore and to develop oil fields in the Kazakh part of the Caspian Sea. In early July, the prosecutor's office notified *SolDat* that it was launching an investigation into an allegedly defamatory 30 May article, 'Decembrists accuse Nazarbayev', which it had reprinted from www.eurasia.org.ru. The article held the president responsible for violent ethnic clashes in Almaty in December 1986. The next day, customs officials seized the newspaper's entire print run at the Russian-Kazakh border and arrested Bapi, who was accompanying the shipment. The editor was held in custody for a few hours and then released. *SolDat* had been printing in Russia since local printing companies started refusing to print the paper a month earlier. Investigators have frozen the newspaper's bank accounts and, as a result, *SolDat*'s entire staff was placed on indefinite unpaid leave from 10 July. (CPJ)

KYRGYZSTAN

On 19 June Jalabad city court jailed independent journalist **Moldosali Ibrahimov** for two years for libel in an article he contributed to the 13 April edition of the state-owned weekly *Akikat*. Both Ibrahimov and Akikat were fined 100,000 soms (about US$1,230). The article, 'Has the judge committed a crime?', described the conduct of a earlier trial and alleged that Judge Toktosun Kasymbekov had accepted a bribe of US$15,000 from Turdubek Chekiev to rule in his favour against Marat Bakiev. The two men were rival parliamentary. Ibrahimov was arrested after the verdict and taken into detention. After five weeks in

jail, Ibrahimov was released on 24 July, at an appeal hearing where his fine was reduced to 10,000 soms. (Osh Media Resource Centre, Azerbaijan Trade Union of Journalists, CPJ, RSF, Internews)

Svetlana Krasilnikova, assistant editor of the independent newspaper *Delo N* (*Index* 3/2000, 4/2000), was hospitalised for investigation of a heart condition on 17 August after an eight-hour interrogation at the Ministry of National Security (MNS). Krasilnikova, editor-in-chief **Viktor Zapolsky** and journalist **Vadim Notchevkin** had been summoned for questioning as part of proceedings against *Delo N* for 'divulging state secrets' by printing the full name of an MNS secret agent. Zapolsky says the information had already been published in state-run newspapers. (GDF, RSF)

Turdakun Usubaliev, member of parliament and former First Secretary of the Central Committee of Kyrgzstan Communist Party, is suing the opposition weekly *Asaba* and its owner, **Melis Eshimkanov**, who is also a presidential candidate. Usubaliev is demanding compensation of 50 million soms (US$1m) on the grounds that the paper has insulted him regularly for the last eight years. The editorial board of *Asaba* say the authorities want to silence the paper ahead of presidential elections set for 29 October. (RFE/RL)

The publication of opposition newspaper *Res Publica* has been resumed. The publication was fined 200,000 soms (US$6,670) for insulting the honour and dignity of

Amanbek Karypkulov, president of the National Television and Radio Corporation (*Index* 2/2000). (RFE/RL)

LIBERIA

Staff of the *New Democrat* have been subjected to repeated threats by government officials and security personnel, while potential advertisers have been warned not to do business with the paper, it was reported on 18 July. As a consequence the *New Democrat* has ceased production and many of its journalists are in hiding. The authorities accused the newspaper of publishing information on the Internet detrimental to the country's reputation. (WAN)

MALAWI

On 10 July **Pushpa Jamieson**, a photographer for the *Chronicle* newspaper, had her camera seized by police while taking pictures of clashes between security forces and protestors at celebrations in Lilongwe to mark the 36th anniversary of independence. The *Chronicle* offices were later surrounded by police, who proceeded to beat journalist **Don Kulapani** when he requested that Jamieson's camera be returned. Kulapani was rescued by colleagues, but police reinforcements arrived and threatened to shoot the corps of journalists if they continued to challenge their 'authority'. (MISA)

On 18 July the millionaire owner of Farmer's World business, Pramod Kalaria, attempted to buy up every copy of the *Chronicle* after an article in that week's edition alleged he had illegally imported workers from India to work on his farms. Vendors in Lilongwe reported that groups of men marauded around town all day, hunting down copies and purchasing them 'lock, stock and barrel'. (MISA)

Prosecutors withdrew charges against *Malawi News* editor **Harace Somanje** and reporter **Mabvuto Banda** on 9 August. The two had been accused of 'conduct likely to breach the peace' after they denounced the government and called on the army to launch a coup (*Index* 5/1999). The authorities offered no apology for the torture meted out to the two men while they were in police custody. (MISA)

MAURITANIA

Copies of the 3 July issue of the private *La Tribune* newspaper were seized by the authorities on the day of publication, because of an interview with an exiled former army colonel who expressed views critical of the government. There was also an article on the expulsion on 1 July of two French citizens, one a diplomat, and an editorial on police violence. Article 11 of the press law permits the seizure of publications 'which threaten the principles of Islam, the credibility of the state, are against the public interest or threaten national security'. (WAN)

MEXICO

Lilly Téllez, a reporter for TV Azteca, was travelling home on the evening of 22 June when her cavalcade met with a volley of bullets. Téllez, who has spearheaded a high-profile

investigation into drug trafficking, escaped injury, but her chauffeur and two bodyguards were wounded. (CPJ)

A report issued by the Federal Electoral Institute (IFE) notes that successful presidential candidate **Vicente Fox** received a disproportionate amount of negative publicity in the media during the June election campaign. The IFE attributed this largely to threats made by the ruling Party of Institutional Revolution, warning newspapers that advertising revenue would be withdrawn if articles favouring Fox were printed. (CPJ)

The body of kidnapped publisher **Hugo Sanchez Eustaquio** was discovered on 19 July, more than three months after he disappeared. Eustaquio worked on the newspaper *La Verdad* in Antizapan de Zaragoza. (IAPA)

On 15 July **Freddy Secundino Sánchez**, a writer for the political magazine *Epoca*, was kidnapped and pistol-whipped by men claiming to be police officers. Sánchez was told by his abductors 'think of those you have dragged through the mud in your bloody magazine ... they sent us to finish you off'. Sánchez, who was covering the presidential elections for the magazine, was released after being warned not to report the incident. (RSF, AI)

The owner of *El Debate de Sinaloa* newspaper was kidnapped on 2 August and held for four days by his captors. **Salido Ibarra** was released unharmed, but news organisations claim that the incident has injured their

campaigns to introduce greater press freedom. (IAPA)

On 15 August the offices of *El Universal* columnist **Ricardo Alemán** were attacked by unknown gunmen. The offices were empty at the time, and the building sustained only light damage from the gunshots. Alemán is known to have angered the Catholic constituency after one piece criticising the Church's attitude to abortion and another condemning the destruction of 'heretical' works of art were printed in early August. (RSF)

MOLDOVA

Freelance investigative reporter **Andrei Turcanu**, known for his work on corruption, has received anonymous telephone calls threatening him and his family with 'extermination' following an article published on 30 June in the Chisinau publication *Messagerul* on the misappropriation of funds by Communist Party members in the privatisation of the tobacco industry. *Messagerul* supports the opposition Party of Democratic Forces and Turcanu, who regularly contributes to the newspaper, has written on government corruption in parliament, the president's office and the cabinet. (RFE/RL, WAN)

MOROCCO

Joseph Tual, a journalist for France 3 television station, was continually harassed by security services during a visit to Morocco from 3 to 9 June. Tual was reporting on the ongoing investigation into the assassination of socialist party leader **Ben Barka**. Plain-clothed police officers shadowed Tual's every move, subjecting him to a number of unnecessary searches and confiscating video cassettes found about his person. (RSF)

The catalogue of banned journals (*Index* 3/2000) grew in early July following the suppression of weekly newspaper *Al Ousboue wa al-Sahafi*. Police officers stormed the Casablanca printing press where the paper was being published on the night of 6 July, ordering printing to cease and arranging for copies to be pulped. It is not known what prompted the action, but the quashing of the paper is thought to be connected with the conviction of *Al Ousboue* editor **Mustapha Alaoui** last month for libel (*Index* 4/2000). (RSF)

Islamic opposition party Al Adl Wal Ihsane announced on 1 August the launch of three websites designed to circumvent an official ban on the organisation's newspapers. The government banned the papers as part of its campaign to control the activity of radical Muslim groups. (*International Herald Tribune*)

NAMIBIA

On 5 July President Sam Nujoma declared his intention to sue the weekly *Windhoek Observer* for reporting on 3 July that he owned a diamond mine in the Democratic Republic of Congo and had involved Namibia in the civil war for personal economic gain. Foreign Affairs Minister Tuliameni Kalomoh described the piece in the *Observer* as the product of a person with a 'peculiarly sick mind'. (MISA)

A fishing company threatened on 23 July to sue the *Windhoek Observer* unless it divulged the source of report that the Gendev firm had allowed contaminated tins of fish to be sold. The company does not deny the allegations, but it is determined to discover the source of the story. (MISA)

The Namibian continued to report on the banning of protest marches in Windhoek. On 6 August, two marches – one by a student organisation, and another by a group of Swaziland dissidents – were prevented from going ahead by police officers, who threatened to arrest participants 'if they moved a metre'. (MISA)

NIGER

Dauda Traore, editor-in-chief of the private weekly *Carnado*, was arrested and detained on 22 June by officers from Niamey's Criminal Investigation Department. The next day **Abdoulaye Tchiénogo,** managing editor of the publication, was also detained. In August 1999 the authorities suspended the weekly for three months and the paper's editor-in-chief was detained for several hours. (RSF)

On 27 June a Niamey magistrates court dismissed a libel suit filed by Prime Minister Hama Amadou for an article which described him as 'pyromaniac but coward'. Less than a week later, after a 30-minute hearing, another court dismissed for procedural irregularity a libel case filed by the army chief of staff against the satirical newspaper, *Le Concord Libéré*. The action was brought on the grounds that an article sought to 'undermine the moral of the troops' and 'incite the

army to disobedience'. (RSF)

NIGERIA

On 9 June police in Abuja attacked **Ken Enseni** and cameraman **Wale Fatoye** of the private Minaj Broadcasting International (MBI) as they began filming a spontaneous demonstration protesting against a recent fuel price hike. Police beat the journalists, arrested them, and interrogated them at the Wuse police station in Abuja. When released several hours later, Enseni and Fatoye checked themselves into Iduma Specialist Hospital for treatment of bruises, cuts and head trauma. (Independent Journalism Centre)

In a letter on 26 June, the commissioner of police in Anambra state directed the Nigerian Union of Journalists to 'produce' **Tony Edike**, local correspondent of *Vanguard* newspaper, for interview by the authorities on 27 June. Two policemen, who did not give their names, warned that Edike should honour the invitation 'in his own interest, or face problems with the police'. (Independent Journalism Centre)

Governor Ahmed Sani of Zamfara State has banned the broadcast of anti-*sharia* items on state radio. The governor, who disclosed this in an interview with the British Broadcasting Corporation (BBC) in early July, advised those who held opposing views on the controversial Islamic legal system to 'go elsewhere to air those views'. (Independent Journalism Centre).

On 5 July veteran female reporter

Funmi Komolafe, of the private daily *Vanguard*, and a cameraman with Murhi International Television (MITV) were severely beaten up by a group of striking union workers at the Alausa State Secretariat building in Lagos. Komolafe who is well known for her coverage of organised labour, was due to interview an official from the Nigeria Labour Congress. But the two media workers were mistaken for reporters from Lagos Television, which the assailants claimed had been biased in its reports on their dispute with the state government. (Independent Journalism Centre)

PAKISTAN

On 21 June Lt-General (retired) Muhammad Shafiq, governor of the North West Frontier Province, announced a ban on cable television networks while addressing a meeting of religious leaders. According to local press reports, the governor's order followed the speeches of several Muslim clerics who said that the networks spread obscenity and vulgarity in the province. On 22 June Shafiq's spokesman clarified that the governor had only been referring to illegal and pirate networks and not to 'authorised' ones. (Pakistan Press Foundation)

In late June **Saeed Zaman Afridi**, a correspondent for the *News*, was arrested in Khyber Agency after his insistence on covering a militia operation in the district led to an argument with an officer of the paramilitary Rangers. (Pakistan Press Foundation)

Inayat-ul-Haq Yasini, a journalist with the daily *Wahdat* in

Peshawar, received anonymous threats over the phone on 4 July. In its 26 June issue, *Wahdat* published a survey by Yasini based on the comments of Afghan refugees and their leaders. The anonymous caller objected to the article bcause he thought it was too favourable to General Al-Maroof Shariati, leader of the exiled Afghanistan National Council for Peace party. A number of prominent Afghan exiles have been intimidated or attacked in recent months (*Index* 4/2000). (RSF)

On 10 July policemen entered the Lahore Press Club while **Omer Ailya**, leader of a traders' movement which has protested strongly against the military government's economic policy, was giving a press conference. Several journalists were beaten by the police after they tried to prevent officers from entering the building, and Ailya was arrested and taken to Karachi. (RSF)

On 6 August the publishing licence of the daily *Inquilab* was cancelled by the district magistrate of the city of Quetta, Baluchistan province. The reason given was the paper's alleged 4 June publication of 'false and fabricated news' against the province's chief secretary. The owner of the newspaper plans to appeal. (Pakistan Press Foundation)

Zahid Amin Orakzai, correspondent for the Islamabad-based Urdu daily *Khabrian* in Kohat district, was arrested on 9 August by order of the district administration. The local government has accused Orakzai of writing a 7 August article in which he reported that men and women were 'mixed' during a concert

organised by the authorities for Independence Day. (RSF)

PANAMA

Jean Marcel Chéry, a journalist at *El Panamá América* newspaper, was convicted of 'criminal defamation' on 14 July and sentenced to 18 months' imprisonment. The sentence referred to a 1996 article in which Chéry accused the police of embezzling stolen jewellery recovered from criminals. (CPJ)

The homes of three *La Prensa* journalists were surrounded by armed police on 9 August after they absconded from trial. Director **Gustavo Gorriti** (*Index* 5/1997, 1/1998. 2/1998, 1/2000) and reporters **Rolando Rodríguez** (*Index* 2/1998) and **Mónica Palm** were charged with 'defaming' Attorney-General José Antonio Sossa. The three are being prosecuted in relation to an article published in *La Prensa* that claimed Sossa has connections with US drug traffickers. Sossa has been the subject of a catalogue of media investigations in recent months, but has used his position as attorney-general to turn the tables on his accusers. On 23 June he sentenced the editor of the daily *El Siglo*, **Carlos Singares**, to eight days in prison for alleging that he frequented brothels. (CPJ)

PARAGUAY

On 21 July the telecommunications regulatory board CONATEL ordered the seizure of the broadcasting equipment of 'pirate' radio station FM Trinidad. Following protests from community radio groups, CONATEL suspended the auction

ANWAR IQBAL
They changed my God

I do not know how God is related to me.
Is it love and respect that links me to Him?
Or fear that forces me to seek his refuge?
Is He a loving friend or a cruel ruler?
Is He like a cloud that protects us from the scorching sun?
Or is he the fire that burns us?

I still love him, even after so many years.
I cannot forget the time I spent with Him,
That's when we were friends – me and my God.
We roamed around together, holding hands,
Collecting feathers of coloured birds,
Exotic flowers, ran after butterflies,
And spent hours in friendly chats.

But they came and took my God away from me
And changed him.

They came shouting:
'We cannot led God waste his time.
We are here to save him from kids and butterflies.
He has more important things to do.
Give him to us!'

They lifted God on their shoulders and
Walked out of my garden, chanting slogans,

They bring all his orders to us and say,
'This is what God says. Do it!'
Those who do not
Are kicked, beaten up, flogged and even killed,
All in the name of God.... ❏

*Pakistani poet **Anwar Iqbal** was threatened with death by an unidentified Islamist group after reciting the Urdu original of this abridged poem in Islamabad in late July. The full version of the poem is available at* www.indexoncensorship.org

for 60 days on 25 July to discuss ways of democratising the process. (Paraguayan Union of Journalists, AMARC)

PERU

Investigative journalist **Monica Vecco** of the daily *La República* received a threatening email on 8 June after writing a critical article on the ruling party, Peru 2000. The message was sent by the Fifth of April Group, a pro-government extremist organisation named after President Alberto Fujimori's coup in April 1992. Vecco's investigative piece looked into the alleged use by Peru 2000 of a workshop belonging to a National Intelligence Service official for printing electoral propaganda. (AI, IPYS)

A congress member has accused daily *El Comercio* and TV station Canal N of breaking the law during an investigation into alleged electoral fraud by ruling party, Peru 2000. On 2 July *El Comercio* editor **Alejandro Miró Quesada** denounced the accusation as another attempt by the government to intimidate the daily and TV station for the damaging disclosure of Peru 2000's alleged use of bogus signatures to get on the electoral register. Ruling party congresswoman Edith Mellado said that a conversation taped between a reporter and an electoral official during the investigation was 'telephone tapping' and therefore illegal. (IPYS)

Cuzco-based radio journalist **Luis Baltazar Caviedes Nuñez de la Torre** died after being severely beaten around the head on 2 July in mysterious circumstances.

Caviedes, who founded a local branch of the National Association of Journalists, was found unconscious on a river bank with severe bruises on the right side of his head and face. He died after being driven to hospital. Caviedes worked for radio stations Sur Oriente and Frecuencia Integral in Quillabamba, Cuzco. (IFJ)

Radio journalist **José del Carmen Parraguez Pérez** was beaten up by unidentified assailants on 4 July outside the city hall of Nueva Cajamarca in north-eastern Peru. The attackers threatened to kill Parraguez before running off. The journalist, who hosts news programme *Análisis* on FVC radio station, had been threatened on previous occasions for reporting on local government corruption cases (IFJ)

Press helicopters were prevented from providing aerial coverage of a demonstration against President Fujimori's controversial election to a third term after the Peruvian Air Force imposed 'restrictions' on civilian flights over Lima's airspace between 25 and 29 July. The three-day protest, led by opposition leader **Alejandro Toledo**, kicked off on 26 July to coincide with Fujimori's swearing-in ceremony on 28 July. A helicopter recently bought by independent cable news station Canal N to cover the protests remained grounded. (CPJ, IPYS)

Around 16 journalists from local and foreign media were attacked during anti-government demonstrations in Lima on 28 July. Some were perpetrated by police, some by demonstrators and others by what were described as

'criminal infiltrators'. Among those assaulted were photo-journalists **Virgilio Grajeda**, **Luis Gonzáles** and **Guillermo Venegas** of daily *La República*; **Miguel Carrillo** and **José Tejada** of *Etecé* magazine; **Roberto Silva** of radio network RPP; **Fidel Carrillo** of daily *Liberación*; **Luis Choy** and **Carlos Lezama** of daily *Ojo*; **José Ibarra** of *La Industria de Trujillo*; and **Rosario Vicentello** of Canal A. Also attacked were **Erika Montalvo**, **Francisco Zacarías** and **Sergio Cuervo** of Colombian TV station Cadena Caracol; **Paul Vanotti** of US news agency Public Media Center; and **Jaime Rázuri** of Agence France Press. Most were beaten or hit by flying objects, and many had equipment stolen or destroyed. A number of TV and radio studios, including those of Canal 4, Canal 5 and RPP, were targeted by ransacking mobs. Canal 9's mobile unit was also attacked. Assailants drove off with the van and transmission equipment after beating the driver. (IPYS, IFJ)

Opposition daily *Liberación* faces yet another threat after being issued on 9 August with a US$1m libel suit from Manuel Alberto Ulloa Van Peborgh, executive director of Editora Nacional which publishes the *Expreso* and *Extra* dailies. Named in the suit are *Liberación's* editor-in-chief, **César Hildebrandt** (*Index* 2/1998, 4/1998, 4/1999, 6/1999, 2/2000, 3/2000), journalist **Mariela Patriau** and columnist **Fernando Viaña**. The latter is the former general manager of *Liberación's* publishing house, BDHIV, leading some lawyers to believe that he was included in the suit to do maximum damage to the daily by ensuring its equipment and assets can be confiscated. Ulloa Van Peborgh is claiming defamation for an article published late last year by *Liberación* on the circumstances surrounding his father's death. (IPYS, IFJ)

PHILIPPINES

An armed group ambushed the car of radio commentator **Roy David** from the GV-FM station in Angeles City, Pampanga Province on 26 June. Three people were killed and David was seriously injured. David and his co-hosts, **Ody Fabian** and **Bong Lacson**, on the programme *Politics and others* had criticised *jueteng*, 'Lord Bong Pineda' and Pampanga Governor Lapid. *Jueteng* is an illegal numbers game which flourishes under police and local official protection in the province. (RSF)

It was reported on 27 June that **Vincent Rodriguez**, a correspondent of the DZMM radio station in Pampanga, was shot dead as he covered the visit of President Joseph Estrada's son, Jojo Osorio Ejercito, to the province on 23 May. The killers, who were targeting Ejercito, are believed to be rebels from Rebolusyonaryong Bayan (RHB), a breakaway faction of the communist New People's Army. (RSF)

Following the abduction of 21 foreign tourists from a Malaysian resort by Jolo-based Muslim guerrilla group Abu Sayyaf on 23 April, it is believed that more than 30 hostages are being held, including five foreign journalists. On 2 July **Andreas Lonrenz**, correspondent for the German weekly *Der Speigel*, was abducted and held incommunicado for 25 days by a splinter faction of Abu Sayyaf and released on 27 July. On 9 July, rebels kidnapped **Maryse Burgot, Jean-Jacques Le Garrec** and **Roland Madura**, journalists from the television station France 2, who were also on Jolo trying to get interviews with the hostages. On 24 July two local journalists, **Val Cuenca** and **Maan Macapagal** from the Philippine Network ABS-CBN, were kidnapped from Upper Kahunayan, an area controlled by Abu Sayyaf, and released on 29 July. (Associated Press, CPJ, Reuters, RSF, WAN, IPI)

PUERTO RICO

On 22 June US navy personnel detained three journalists covering a protest against the stationing of US troops on Vieques Island **Walter Leon** and **Edmundo Cid** of Canal 4 and **Aidsé Maldonado** of *El Horizonte* were accused of illegal trespassing and delivered to a federal court, where they were given a severe reprimand for their conduct. (IAPA)

RUSSIA

Media-Most group owner **Vladimir Gusinsky**, who was held for investigation into alleged fraud charges following a raid on his offices in Moscow in May (*Index* 4/2000), was arrested again on 13 June on suspicion of embezzlement and held in Moscow's Butyrskaya jail. The charge related to the purchase of a state-owned television station in St Petersburg in the mid-1990s. All charges were denied by Gusinsky's lawyers. (IPI, WPFC, GDF)

French photographer **Brice Fleutiaux,** who had been detained in Chechnya for eight months (*Index* 1/2000), was released on 12 June after Russian authorities declared that his kidnapping was a 'warning to all journalists wanting to enter Chechnya without military authorisation'. (RSF)

The authorities are questioning Chechen journalist **Taisa Isaeva** over her alleged involvement in the abduction of a Moscow TV crew and two British charity workers in 1997. The 29-year-old had worked as a journalist for Chechen state TV's cultural channel, Nokhcho, until it closed last year, but she denied any connection with the Chechen propaganda ministry. (Institute of War and Peace Reporting)

An article called 'Ripped Elections' in Issue 29 of the newspaper *Arsenievskie Vesti* in eastern Primorsk led to the imprisonment of editor-in-chief **Irina Grebneva** for five days after she was found guilty by Judge L. Vedjun of 'slight hooliganism'. Grebneva wrote the article and included quotations from Vladivostok Governor Evgenij Nazdratenko's speeches without any deletions even though many words and phrases were supposedly 'unprintable'. (GDF)

Sergei Novikov, owner of the independent Vesna radio station in Smolensk Province, east of Moscow, was killed in the late evening of 26 July. Novikov had left the station with a friend and entered his apartment building where an unidentified person shot him four times on the stairwell before escaping through the back. In the past the radio station aired allegations of corruption in the regional administration and Novikov had participated in a television broadcast during which he and other local journalists discussed the alleged corruption of the provincial deputy governor. (IPI, RSF).

Igor Domnikov died on 16 July in Burdenko Neurosurgical Institute as a result of injuries sustained in a hammer attack in his apartment in south-east Moscow on 12 May (*Index* 4/2000). He did not regain consciousness. The 42-year-old journalist, who covered cultural and social issues for the twice-weekly independent newspaper *Novaya Gazeta*, is believed to have been mistaken for a colleague, **Oleg Sultanov**, who lived in the same block. Sultanov had been investigating corruption within the minerals industry and had already received threats from the security services. (RSF, WAN, CPJ, Centre for Journalism in Extreme Situations)

Radio journalist **Andrei Babitsky**, who 'disappeared' in Chechnya in mid-January (*Index* 2/2000, 3/2000), was formally charged on 6 August with 'knowingly using false identity papers'. Babitsky testified that he had been exchanged by the authorities against his will for Russian soldiers. Regarding his forged documentation, Babitsky claimed that his Chechen captors had forced him to agree to go to Azerbaijan and had taken his passport and ID. They forged an Azeri passport for him but had forgotten that he needed an Azeri border pass. Babitsky said he was driven to Dagestan and forced to check into a hotel with his forged passport and was subsequently

arrested by the Dagestan authorities during a routine check of all documents of hotel residents. If found guilty, Babitsky could face up to six months in prison. (WIPC, RSF)

SAMOA

The Supreme Court ruled on 3 August that opposition members of parliament be allowed free access to government media. The late prime minister, Tofilau Eti Alesana, had restricted opposition access to national broadcaster Radio 2AP and Televise Samoa during his mandate. (PINA)

SERBIA-MONTENEGRO

Journalist **Dusica Radulovic**, director of *Borske Novine* newspaper in Bor, was sentenced to three months in jail on 2 June for a series of articles published between January 1997 and January 1998 which were said to libel municipal officials. Her husband, **Miroslav Radulovic**, the editor-in-chief of *Borske Novine*, is currently on trial for a photomontage of President Slobodan Milosevic. (WAN, WPC)

Radio Kontakt journalist and editor **Valentina Cukic** was shot in the chest and seriously wounded on 20 June in central Belgrade outside the Radio Television Kosovo building. At the time of the attack Cukic was wearing Kosovo Stabilisation Force (KFOR) press credentials which clearly identified her as a journalist. The station, which broadcasts in several languages, was the target of a rocket-propelled attack on 17 April. (CPJ, RSF)

Followers of the unrecognised Montenegrin Orthodox Church assaulted FoNet photographer **Zivots Ciric** in the village of Njegusi on 10 July for no apparent reason. His camera was broken by a church official's bodyguards and, after leading him away, police exposed Circi's film to the light. (RFE/RL, ANEM)

During the celebrations of the satirical weekly *Nasa Krmaca*'s fourth anniversary on 11 July, editor-in-chief **Bosko Savkovic** announced that the publication would close after producing 80 issues, six special editions and 14 books. He said that staff had suffered pressure both from the government and the opposition, which felt *Nasa Krmaca*'s existence reinforced the 'illusion of press freedom'. Savkovic explained that new pressures, including the lack of newsprint and changes in legislation, were the reasons for its closure. (RFE/RL, ANEM)

The families of five victims of the NATO bomb attack on Radio Television Serbia have laid charges against European governments in the European Court of Human Rights, it was reported on 17 July. A British law firm involved in the case stated that there was sufficient evidence to demonstrate that European governments had committed war crimes by bombing a non-military target. (Free B2-92)

On 20 July Information Minister Goran Matic said his government viewed Radio Free Europe/Radio Liberty as a propaganda arm of the NATO coalition and refused to register its bureau in Belgrade. (RFE/RL)

Kraljevo journalist **Miroslav Filipovic**, who wrote for the independent *Danas* paper, Agence France-Presse and the Institute for War and Peace Reporting, was sentenced to seven years' imprisonment by the Nis Military Court on 26 July for espionage and disseminating false information (*Index* 4/2000). The charges concerned a report on alleged massacres of ethnic Albanian civilians, indiscriminate shelling of villages and looting by Serb troops and paramilitaries during NATO's bombing campaign in Kosovo in 1999. The trial was conducted behind closed doors within two days. (IPI, IFJ, IWPR)

After refusing to pay a fine of DM25,000, the Albanian-language daily *Dita* based in Pristina was ordered to cease publication on 27 July by Douglas Davidson, acting media commissioner of the OSCE, The fine was initially imposed after the newspaper published an article on 4 July which carried names and photographs of 15 Serbs who had allegedly committed war crimes in Kosovo. *Dita* was previously suspended by the UN mission in Kosovo after publishing similar material about a Serb employee who was later found murdered (*Index* 4/2000). (ANEM)

The independent daily *Danas* was fined 200,0000 dinars (cUS$17,850) on 9 August and one of its journalist, **Veseljko Koprivica**, received a fine of 70,000 dinars under the Public Information Law. Vice Prime Minister Vojislav Seselj, president of the Radical Party, filed a complaint against *Danas* following the newspaper's 4 August publication of a press release by the

opposition party Democracy Alternative. It stated that, although Seselj had promised not to run in the presidential election, he had eight million posters printed by a Belgrade-based company. The printing house for the newspaper, Dan Graf, was also fined 200,000 dinars and its director, **Dusan Mitrovic**, was fined 70,000 dinars in connection with the same article. (RSF, Radio B2-92, ANEM, RFE/RL)

A bomb exploded under the car of journalist **Bora Odalovic** outside his residence in the northern Montenegrin city of Niksic on 3 August. It was unoccupied and police believed that the journalist was not the intended victim. (ANEM)

Cedomir Jovanovic, a Democratic Party official, was sentenced to five months in prison with three years' probation on 3 August for 'damaging the reputation of state officials'. The charges were laid by Deputy Minister for Information Radmila Visic over articles in the bulletin *Promene,* published by ABC Grafika during the Alliance for Change protests in Belgrade in October last year. ABC Grafika and Jovanovic were fined a total amount of about 3m dinars. (ANEM)

Misdemeanour charges against **Dragan Hadzi**, director of the state-run daily *Politika*, and **Lazar Milicevic**, the paper's Mladenovac correspondent, have been filed by Predrag Nikodijevic, director of the Bureau for Construction and Planning in the outer Belgrade suburb of Mladenovac. It was reported on 31 July that the charges related to the publication of an

article on 25 July, entitled 'Local construction bureau distributing solidarity apartments illegally', which Nikodijvic claims contained false information. (ANEM)

SIERRA LEONE

On 14 June **Author Caulker** a journalist with the private bi-weekly *Salone Times*, was kicked repeatedly by Major Umar, a Nigerian officer serving with the UNAMSIL peace-keeping force. The attack followed an article on 9 May which condemned a UNAMSIL commander for firing a warning shot in the presence of demonstrators outside the house of RUF leader Foday Sankoh. According to the article, the warning shot 'gave the green light to the sporadic gunshots fired by the [rebel] combatants' into the crowd, which led to the death of more than 20 people. (RSF).

SOLOMON ISLANDS

The *Solomon Star* was banned on 5 June from sale in three provincial towns of Western Province because of anger over the newspaper's 'clear bias' towards the Malaita Eagle Force (MEF), one of the two conflicting ethnic groups on Guadalcanal Island. (Pacific Media Watch)

SOMALIA

Mohamed Abdulkadir Ahmed, editor-in-chief of the private weekly *Sahan*, was arrested in Bossasso in the regional state of Puntland and imprisoned, it was reported on 17 July. He was beaten by police and taken to the town's port where he was forced into a container. His arrest followed the publication of articles that supported the ongoing peace talks hosted in Djibouti and criticised the Putland government for boycotting the conference. (WAN)

SOUTH AFRICA

It was reported in late June that the ANC is considering withholding state advertising revenue from 'hostile' media organisations. An ANC source was quoted as saying: 'The state possesses huge resources which it invests in different media organisations ... such investments cannot be allowed to prop up forces and institutions that promote the very opposite of what the democratic state stands for'. (*Southern Africa Report*)

Freelance journalist **Dale McKinley** was expelled from the Communist Party on 15 August for criticising the party's alliance with the ruling ANC. McKinley, who was chairman of the party's Johannesburg branch, accused the leadership of abandoning its principles by denying freedom of expression. (Freedom of Expression Institute)

SOUTH KOREA

Kim In-gu, a reporter with the daily *Chosun Ilbo*, was refused entry into North Korea on 27 June despite being on a list of six journalists invited to cover a meeting on reunification between the Red Cross Societies of both countries. He was accused of writing 'offending articles' about North Korea. Radio Pyongyang threatened on 8 July to 'blow up' the offices of *Chosun Ilbo* in Seoul, calling its journalists 'confrontational maniacs, liars and

traitors'. (RSF)

SRI LANKA

The Supreme Court ruled on 30 June that the censorship the government had imposed on 3 May this year (*Index* 4/2000) is illegal. The judgment follows a fundamental rights application filed by the *Sunday Leader* challenging the Competent Authority (CA) Ariya Rubasinghe's order to seal the printing press of Leader Publications on 22 May. The three judges ruled that the order issued by Rubasinghe against the group was illegal because the emergency regulations did not specify 'who the CA should be'. The court also ruled that the recently imposed emergency regulations had not empowered President Kumaratunga to appoint a CA to impose censorship. Nonetheless, the government reimposed censorship on 'military information' by formally appointing Rubasinghe as the Competent Authority, or chief censor, on 3 July. Journalists no longer have to send in all of their copy prior to publication, but they will be held liable if they are found guilty of publishing material that undermines the armed forces, or is 'prejudicial to the interests of national security or the preservation of public order'. (CPJ, RSF, Asian Human Rights Commission, IPI, Reuters)

On 18 July the public harassment campaign against **Roy Denish**, **Saman Wagaarachchi**, **P Sivaram** and **P Seevagan** (*Index* 4/2000) continued when the four journalists were alleged to have 'betrayed the country to the [Tamil] Tigers' in an article in the

pro-government newspaper *Jana Ravaya*. (RSF)

On 21 July the government banned the showing of **Prasanna Vithanage**'s award-winning anti-war film *Purasanda Kaluwara* (Death on a Full Moon Day) on the grounds that the prevailing security situation was not 'ideal' for the film's release. (Free Media Movement, BBC World Service)

Recent Publication: *New Emergency Regulations – erosion of human rights protection* (AI, July 2000, pp 17)

SUDAN

It was reported on 11 July that the National Press Council (NPC) had suspended the Tuesday edition of independent Arabic daily *al-Rai al-Aam* as a penalty for publishing an article critical of the police. The suspension was reported by the government-owned *al-Anbaa* which said the NPC made the decision following a complaint of defamation. The article had criticised police for forcing people to conform to Islamic ideals as prescribed by President Omar Beshir. (Deutsche Press Agentur)

Hassan Ahmed Osman was rearrested on 17 July at his office in Khartoum, allegedly for his activities as a communist activist. He was previously arrested on 10 July and his personal computer and printer were confiscated by the security forces. (Sudanese Victims of Torture Group)

SWAZILAND

Forced out of his job at *Times Sunday* last September, the paper's former editor, **Bheki Makhubu**,

• •

HAMZI MUSTAFA NJOZI
Sure-footed slaughter

It was on the afternoon of Friday 13 February, 1998 that armed policemen were ordered to open fire at the people who were outside the Mwembechai mosque.

From the videotape of the shooting it's clear at least four people were killed and many others maimed. It is also quite obvious from the tape that the aim was to kill the Muslims. On the tape the police commanders are seen and heard ordering their marksmen to take careful aim of their targets. In two cases the first bullets wounded without killing the intended victims, and the police commander in both cases ordered his men to shoot again. And they did, with unmistakable zest and ruthlessness. The tape also shows the police dragging the bodies of the dead and throwing them into the lorries.

There is one brief scene in this tape which always moves me to tears. The commander orders a young policeman to shoot. He shoots in the air. The commander orders him to aim his gun at the crowd. The young policeman is clearly torn between obeying his commander and obeying his conscience. The commander repeats the order. The policeman makes a brave attempt to obey his commander. He raises his gun, he looks at the crowd, but his hands become weaker and weaker, and the gun slowly falls to the ground.

Was he a Muslim? Or a Christian whose conscience revolted against the idea of killing innocent human beings? I guess his name was not in the list of those policemen who were later to be praised and promoted for their fine job at Mwembechai. But why was the commander so particular that his policemen should shoot to kill? Why was he so sure of his footing? I do not know, and we may not ever know the truth. ❑

*On 4 August the authorities banned **Hamzi Mustafa Njozi**'s book* Mwembenchai Killings and the Political Future of Tanzania, *which details the massacre of four Muslim youths by police in 1998, allegedly at the instigation of a Catholic priest. Njozi was recently banned from bringing copies of the book, which is published in Canada, into the country. Signed by President Benjamin Mkapa, the order prohibits, with immediate effect, the book's sale or distribution. It is, however, being publicised by the 'Islam in Tanzania' website.*

• •

was charged on 10 July with 'criminal defamation'. Makhubu, who penned an article alleging that Princess Liphovela, the king's bride-to-be, was a high-school drop-out (*Index* 6/1999) – facts that were not in any way disputed – faces a prison sentence if found guilty. (MISA)

TOGO

On three seperate occasions in July police officers confiscated copies of opposition weekly *Combat du Peuple*, following its publication of a report by the Togolese League of Human Rights. A warrant issued on 14 April calling for the arrest of *Combat du Peuple* editor **Lucien Messan** remains outstanding. (RSF)

TUNISIA

Distribution of the French weekly *Jeune Afrique-L'Intelligent* was severely disrupted in early July after its distributor, at the behest of the Ministry of Communications, announced that all government offices, embassies and public companies had cancelled their subscriptions. On 3 July, the paper's management railed against the 'economic censorship' imposed on it following publication of an article critical of the country's human rights record. (RSF)

Moncef Marzouki, spokesman for the National Council on Liberties in Tunisia, was removed on 29 July from his position at the University of Sousse on the orders of the Ministry of Health. Marzouki had vexed the authorities by speaking out against continued repression while on a trip to the United States. (HRW)

On 14 August **Mustapha Ben Jaafar**, secretary general of the Democratic Forum for Employment and Liberties, was detained by state security forces. Ben Jaafar, who published a pamphlet critical of government repression on 3 August, was accused of 'maintenance of an unrecognised association' and 'diffusion of false news'. (Tunisian National Council for Liberties)

TURKEY

On 10 June **Irfan Hosafcioglu**, former chairman of the Journalists Association, and editor-in-chief of local periodical *Dogruyol Gazetesi*, was attacked in the street by unidentified assailants. (RSF)

Ahmet Onal, owner of the Peri Publishing House, has gone on trial facing a sentence of 27 years in jail. Onal was deemed responsible for the publication of a book by writer, **Mahmut Baksi** (*Index* 4/2000), entitled '*The Hawk: Kurdish Businessman, Huseyin Baybasin*'. Now living in the Netherlands, Baybasin was a notorious figure in the narcotics trade and his memoirs expose the links between right-wing Kurdish mafia, the state and the military in drugs trafficking. (Kurdish Observer)

The trial of Dr **Fikret Baskaya** in connection with his article published in the daily *Ozgur Bakis*, concluded on 13 June. Baskaya was sentenced to a fine and one year in prison for disseminating 'separatist propaganda'. (*Yeni Gundem*)

A theatre group in Batman city was banned from performing a play entitled *Hamal* (The Porter) by order of the regional governor, it

was reported on 13 June. **Sadik Aksoy**, author and director of the play, said he could not conceive of any reason for the prohibition. Batman, in the State of Emergency Region, had previously hosted the play and it had been well received, he claimed. (Kurdish Observer)

Hayrettin Celik, correspondent for the Kurdish daily *Yeni Gundem*, was arrested by police in Adana on 14 June and taken to the anti-terror branch of the security police (notorious for their use of torture on suspects). The arrest seemed to be connected to a previous prosecution, when the journalist had been acquitted. He was released the next day. (RSF)

On 17 June a new Kurdish television channel, Mesopotamia TV, was launched in Copenhagen. Mesopotamia is a new satellite channel serving Kurdish language audiences across 77 countries in the Middle East, Europe and North Africa, broadcasting in all main Kurdish dialects. (Info-Turk)

Kamil Tekin Surek, editor with the left-wing daily *Yeni Evrensel* and lawyer for the family of murdered journalist **Metin Goktepe** (*Index* 2/1996, 6/1996, 1/1997, 6/1997, 1/1998, 2/1998, 3/1998, 5/1998, 1/1999, 2/1999, 4/1999, 4/2000), was arrested on 24 June and held for two days. (*Evrensel*)

An issue of the Kurdish weekly *Roja Teze* was seized on 24 June for two articles which contained the terms 'Kurdish movement', 'Kurdistan', 'independent Kurdistan' and 'Kurdish national movement'. (RSF)

An Istanbul court confiscated the

Islamic daily *Akit* on 28 June for inciting hatred and religious discrimination. The incriminating article criticised media adulation of Guven Erkaya, an army member who had violently attacked Islamic circles in 1997. (RSF)

The editor-in-chief of the daily *Cumhuriyet*, **Fikret Ilkiz**, was given a suspended fine in late June for an article about a press conference given by human rights activists in 1999. Ilkiz was accused of 'hindering the course of justice'. (RSF)

Aydin Acar, a singer from Hakkari, was arrested on 30 June after performing at a local wedding. Acar had sung '*Kine Em*' (Who Are We?), written by the Kurdish poet **Cigerxwin**. He was charged with 'separatist propaganda'. (Kurdish Observer)

On 12 July three national TV channels – Kral, Show and Interstar – were suspended for a day by the Supreme Board of Radio and Television for 'undermining family values' by broadcasting and discussing a saucy song. (RSF)

Songul Ozkan, the owner of Evrensel Publishing House, was sentenced in absentia on 12 July to two years in prison and a fine for publishing a booklet entitled 'The Kurdish Question and Democratisation'. Lawyers protested the legality of the decision, and called it 'a hindrance to freedom of expression'. (Kurdish Observer)

Sener Levent, owner and editor-in-chief of *Avrupa* newspaper, and editorial writers **Harun Denizkan** and **Ali Osman Tabak**

were arrested on 8 July for 'espionage activities' and 'attempts to infiltrate military circles'. Two days later, *Avrupa* photographer **Mehmet Inanci** was arrested on the same charges. Seventy-five legal cases have been launched against *Avrupa* in recent months, mainly concerning the paper's critical stance on official policy in Northern Cyprus. (WAN)

The Supreme Board of Radio and Television ordered a one-year suspension of Istanbul radio station Ozgur Radyo on 20 July for broadcasting a verse from a poem by **Ataol Behramoglu** during a programme on 1 May. Behramoglu contested the decision, stating that 'this verse, written 30 years ago, is published in all new editions of my books'. (RSF, Kurdish Media)

On 21 July **Ahmet Coban**, editor-in-chief of the newspaper *Acik Sayfa*, appeared in court on charges that could result in up to six years in prison. As part of an investigation into the corruption of judicial power, the paper had published an ironic article entitled 'There is no corruption in the justice system'. The judge is also considering charging the author of the article, **Adnan Ekinci**. (RSF)

Esen Isil, **Durul Gur**, **Celal Cimen** and **Ozgur Gulbir**, reporters for the TV company Case Productions, were all detained with 22 others inside the Mesopotamian Cultural Centre in Istanbul in late July. The four were producing a report about Istanbul for French-German TV station Arte. They were held for some hours and then released without an explanation. (RSF)

On 30 June the Ashgabat authorities shut down the country's last private Internet and email provider. Efforts continue to save at least 'the shell' of the Ariana Internet Provider (*Index* 4/2000). (RFE/RL)

A body of journalists announced on 18 July that it intended to boycott parliament until laws limiting access to information were lifted. The Parliamentary Press Corps, a lobby representing the media, will impose a news blackout until new legislation preventing reporters from speaking to MPs is repealed. (Digital Freedom Network, Rights Features Service)

The government issued a decree on 18 August prohibiting journalists from interviewing victims of alleged atrocities by the Allied Democratic Forces (ADF) rebel group. The ADF is thought to have tortured and beheaded civilians in the western region. President Yoweri Museveni ordered hospitals to deny journalists access to patients injured by ADF actions, threatening any who disobeyed with immediate arrest. (Digital Freedom Network)

The trial of three senior *Monitor* staff, who were charged in July 1999 with 'sedition' (*Index* 4/1999), will begin on 14 September, it was announced in August. **Wafula Oguttu**, **Charles Onyango-Obbo** and **David Ouma Balikowa** were accused after the daily newspaper carried pictures of a group of soldiers sexually assaulting a woman. The defendants argued that it was the military personnel, not themselves, who should be facing prosecution. (Digital Freedom Network, Rights Features Service)

USA

It was reported on 6 June that nearly twice as many black than white men and women are being imprisoned for drug offences even though, according to studies, there are five times as many white drug users than black ones. (*International Herald Tribune*)

It was reported on 6 June that a television station has been fined for broadcasting information about a victim of a sexual assault which had been stated in open court. KTVQ-TV, of Billings, Montana, was deemed to have violated the 'spirit' of an order imposed by Wyoming District Judge Hunter Patrick and was fined the maximum possible, US$750. (Freedom Forum)

Congress held special hearings at the end of July to discuss Carnivore, the FBI's Internet tapping system. The FBI claims that the software only intercepts emails with origin and destination addresses corresponding to those specifically authorised in a court order, but US experts belive this is impossible because of Internet Service Providers providing their users with a different identification each time they log on. (*Guardian*)

UZBEKISTAN

One of the most popular weeklies, *Darakchi*, disappeared from kiosks in Tashkent on 8 August. No one at the paper could offer an explanation. *Darakchi* first appeared

at independence and was critical of the authorities. (Central Asian News)

VENEZUELA

The editor of weekly *La Razón*, **Pablo López Ulacio**, has had two arrest orders issued against him for refusing to show up in court to answer libel charges filed by a prominent businessman with powerful political connections. López, who is currently in hiding, has also disregarded a court order barring the weekly from publishing any information on the lawsuit. The editor spent five days under house arrest in the first half of July. He was released on 13 July after the judge in charge of the case was found to be biased and was replaced. The new judge, Graudi Villegas, ordered López's arrest again after he ignored another court summons on 4 August. López believes he has no guarantee of getting a fair trial. The plaintiff is Tobías Carrero, a prominent supporter of President Hugo Chávez's bid for re-election and friend of legislative chief Luis Miquilena. Carrero sued *La Razón* for implicating his insurance firm, Multinacional de Seguros, in alleged irregularities in the procurement of government contracts. (CPJ, RSF)

YEMEN

It was reported that on the morning of 5 June that **Arafat Mudabish**, journalist for the daily *Al Ayyam*, was brutally beaten by police just outside the court of appeal while trying to photograph the trial of a morgue murder suspect. The attack was witnessed by 1,000 protesters who were also

being harassed by police. In a press release, Arafat said that the incident was 'brutal and goes against press freedom'. (*Yemen Bulletin*)

On 6 August a Sana court banned **Saif Haderi**, owner and editor-in-chief of the weekly *Al Choumou*, from practising as a journalist for ten months. Haderi was also fined for 'causing damage' to the education minister. (RSF)

ZAMBIA

Parliament is set to pass a bill outlawing legal suits against the state. The new law received its second reading on 3 August and, if implemented, will make it impossible for citizens to seek court injunctions against the state, and prevent aggrieved parties from challenging government decisions. Opponents of the bill have labelled it 'dictatorial'. (Pan Africa News Agency)

Ten *Post* journalists, accused in March 1999 of espionage following the publication of an article questioning the army's capacity to repel a hypothetical Angolan invasion (*Index* 3/1999), were acquitted on 18 August after prosecutors failed to produce solid evidence. Charges against *Post* editor-in-chief **Fred M'membe**, however, were not withdrawn. If M'membe is found guilty, he could face up to 20 years' imprisonment. (MISA)

ZIMBABWE

The Supreme Court has rejected an application by independent radio station Capital Radio to nullify section 27 of the constitution, which positions

Zimbabwe Broadcasting Corporation as the sole radio broadcasting licensee. Capital began broadcasting from outside the country on 13 June. (MISA)

The Supreme Court issued an interim order on 16 June compelling state-owned Zimbabwe Broadcasting Corporation to report the news impartially. The correspondents are now being called upon to explain why a judicial commission should not be established into the matter. (MISA)

Three *Standard* journalists were fined a total of US$473.68 for criminal defamation against the government. Managing director **Clive Wilson**, editor **Andy Moyse** and reporter **Chengetai Zvauya** were sentenced on 20 June over allegations in the *Standard* that the government had printed its draft constitution before public submissions closed. The paper is appealing the verdict. (MISA)

A mob of about 20 ZANU-PF supporters attacked a car carrying foreign journalists in the south on 21 June. Journalists **Beatrice Khadigge** of Agence France-Presse, **Sharon Chetty** of the *Sowetan*, **Guy Oliver** of e-TV and cameraman **Brian Ramapulana** were unhurt in the attack, although the car had its windows broken. (MISA).

Two *Herald* journalists were taken hostage on 7 July while on a visit to the town of Centenary by a group of war veterans. The veterans suspected that **George Soko** and **William Mafunga** were clandestine members of the Movement for Democratic Reform and the two men were 'detained' and ordered to produce their ZANU-PF membership cards to confirm their loyalty to President Robert Mugabe. The war veterans then threatened to beat the journalists and destroy their vehicle. (MISA)

It was revealed on 1 August that the CIA had ordered the assassination of **Geoff Nyarota** editor-in-chief of *Daily News*. The plot was revealed by Bernard Masara, the man hired by the CIA to slay Nyarota with 'a simple weapon'. Masara confessed the conspiracy to *Daily News* staff, and confirmed his story by telephoning his CIA handler and discussing details of the plot in front of the assembled journalists. The *Daily News* has been a scourge of President Mugabe's ZANU-PF government, and it is believed that orders for Nyarota's elimination came 'from the top'. (MISA, *Daily Telegraph*, WAN)

Compiled by: Melanie Clark, Gbenga Oduntan, Shifa Rahman (Africa); Ben Carrdus, Rupert Clayton, Heidi Joyce, Andrew Kendle, Anna Lloyd (Asia); William Escofet (South and Central America); David Gelber, Gill Newsham, Mebrak Tareke (Middle East); Humfrey Hunter (North America and Pacific); Deborah Haynes (UK and western Europe); Katy Sheppard (eastern Europe and the Balkans).

In danger of peace

For almost a quarter of a century, Lebanon has been the proxy battleground for its neighbours as well as the site of a peculiarly destructive civil war. Now, with Israel's withdrawal, the country stands at the crossroads, in danger of the peace that may break out between Israel and the Palestinians

Guest editor, Carol Hakim

CAROL HAKIM

In danger of peace

Lebanon is the land of opposites *par excellence*. Everything and anything in Lebanon defies simple descriptions and explanations: its ancient history, its more modern performance as a nation state, its politics, its social fabric and its culture. Each feature amalgamates and reconciles normally incompatible elements, calling for convoluted and circuitous explications with endless qualifications, digressions and codicils. It is no wonder that foreigners, and even more so its own inhabitants, give up their attempts to make sense of it and eventually take it as it is – or leave it.

Like so many other countries of the third world, its establishment as a modern state was the result of fortuity, contingency and a matter of convenience – for others, of course. Nothing in its past history predisposed it for such a destiny. There are few objective facts or episodes. Such as they are, modern nationalist historians have retrospectively and tardily patched up to compose a coherent and seamless narrative, recounting time and again the story of a small, fierce and determined people which has, since the days of the Phoenicians some 3,000 years ago, struggled to defend its independence. Thereafter, following a rather confused chronology and genealogy, the feats of this refined, urban and maritime people are allegedly carried on by uncouth, mountainous and distrustful populations, who take refuge in the high grounds overlooking the Mediterranean coast to flee from some not always clearly defined danger or oppressor.

Foremost among these communities are the Maronites who, according to differing accounts, established themselves in Mount Lebanon – in the north of the present state – in the seventh century to evade the exactions of the Byzantines or of the Muslims. Then there are the Druze, Arab tribes by descent who, for some indeterminate reason converted in the tenth century to a hermetic and esoteric religion;

followed by the Shiites, another dissident Islamic group, dating back to the seventh century, which splintered from the main Sunnite Islamic core over the issue of the succession to the Prophet Mohammad. Innumerable other arcane eastern Christian communities also settled in Mount Lebanon in the course of history.

The myth-ridden, Lebanese nationalist historical account would not stand any serious scrutiny. Modern Lebanese bear no relation to their alleged Phoenician ancestors, nor did the motley populations who lived in Mount Lebanon ever strive to become a nation, let alone create a state of their own. True, during the Ottoman period, on two occasions, tribal-cum-feudal warlords succeeded in consolidating their rule over the Mountain. Then, in the 19th century, still under Ottoman rule, Mount Lebanon was set up as a semi-autonomous province. However, none of these episodes could in itself account for the creation in 1920 of the independent State of Greater Lebanon. This owed its existence to the designs of the French colonial power entrusted with a mandate over Syria following WWI. Having failed to strike a deal acknowledging French ascendancy in Syria with Faysal, leader of the Arab Revolt, France expelled the Arab Emir and carved up his Syrian dominion into several truncated states in line with the time-honoured colonial precept *divide et impera*. The State of Greater Lebanon, comprising Mount Lebanon proper plus the coastline with Beirut, Tripoli, Sidon and Byblos, as well as the rich Bekaa valley, constituted one of these contrived entities.

Since its establishment, the existence of the State of Lebanon has been contested by one group or another of its inhabitants. Today, some 80 years later, its existence as an independent state is still open to doubt. In between, it has known glorious days and experienced a bitter and implacable 15-year civil and regional war. And all that time, Lebanon has bucked the trend of events in the Middle East. In the 1950s and 60s, for instance, when the Arab world was in the throes of its revolutionary fervour, Lebanon witnessed prosperity and stability. When, in the rest of the Arab world nationalism reigned supreme, promising to sweep away the artificial states established earlier by the colonial powers, Lebanon went on its own way, consolidating its political institutions. Finally, when most of the Arab world embraced socialism and experimented with a controlled economy, Lebanon adopted an unbridled liberal economic system – and got away with it.

This was Lebanon's heyday, when the country prospered and life seemed sweet and easy. Beirut rose to unsurpassed heights to become the main financial, commercial, tourist, educational and cultural hub of the Near East. Its skyscrapers, its luxurious shops, its banks, its restaurants, its night-life, its cultural creativity and, in short, its uninterrupted bustling activity, symbolised its meteoric rise. Money seemed to pour in from all sides. From the West and from the East. Indeed, this miraculous success resided in Lebanon's role as a relay station between the West and the Arab East, channelling the circulation of commodities and capital between the two poles. Western products passed through Lebanon en route to the Arab interior, while Arab capital was deposited in Lebanese banks before being reinvested elsewhere. In the process, Lebanese tradesmen and intermediaries deducted their share of the profits.

At the same time, taking advantage of the unbridled freedom of expression, association and economic activity tolerated in the country, in sharp contrast to the rest of the Arab world where regimes increasingly restricted all unofficial reflection and utterances, the wealthy and cosmopolitan former elites of Egypt, Syria, Iraq and Palestine, as well as the less fortunate intellectuals, radicals and revolutionaries of the Arab world, or mere students from all over the Middle East, attracted by its prestigious universities, flocked into Beirut. The city added another feather to its cap and turned into the intellectual centre of the Middle East. New publishing houses, newspapers, journals sprang up almost daily; intellectual and ideological currents agitating the region at the time came out into the open. If this intellectual effervescence did not really favour a constructive dialogue among all, at the very least a peaceful coexistence, and at times fruitful interaction, prevailed.

However, this glaring affluence did not, and could not last. It rested on too flimsy and fragile a foundation and depended on a specific combination of external factors over which Lebanon had little control. The structural imbalance of the Lebanese economy favoured a highly unequal redistribution of wealth, allowing an increasingly select group of the happy few to grow richer and richer. Structural economic distortions affected the social structure of the country. With the stagnation of agriculture, the rural population thronged to the capital in search of a living which neither the weak industrial sector nor the booming service economy could provide. As a result, many rural migrants ended up in shanty towns, the infamous 'poverty belts' surrounding Beirut. It was the inhabitants of these slums who eventually overran and devastated the capital during the civil war.

Even before the outbreak of the war, the socio-economic flaws started to generate growing tensions. However, the Lebanese political system did not favour the adoption of effective and necessary amendments. Based on a compromise among post-independence notables more preoccupied with the need to preserve their dominant position than with promoting the common good, and on a division of power among the main religious communities of the country, all of which allocated political and administrative posts according to sectarian affiliations rather than competence, the political system was a recipe for disaster. Its inefficiency, patronage and clientelism, political segmentation and endless bargaining among politicians, resulted in shallow makeshift arrangements or, more often than not, stagnation and stalemate. The delicate balance on which the stability of the system depended was sustained by the deliberate avoidance of political debate and consensus while, in reality, the country on the eve of the war was plagued by substantial problems, most notably socio-economic problems, the need for political reform and foreign policy issues.

The system was originally designed to allow a fair and equitable representation of all religious communities, especially the minorities. Its founding fathers had envisaged such a formula rallying the support of all communities for the nascent state; with the passage of time, as solid political institutions took root and as the various sects intermixed and blended into a unified nation, basic distinctions among Lebanon's inhabitants would fade away and the communitarian system fall into disuse. However, the political class, whose vested interests were better served by the perpetuation of the communitarian system, stalled such an evolution. Instead, political communitarianism solidified and helped to intensify the fragmentation of society, its marginalisation and alienation from the political process. Indeed, the system was predicated on a consensus among communal leaders that supposedly denoted the consent of the communities under their control. The Lebanese populations were hence denied direct access to the elitist decision-making process, confined to their original communal communities and deterred from mobilising along different political and social lines.

The Lebanese politicians' lack of concern for socio-economic and political reform was matched by a superb insouciance with regard to mounting regional tensions. 'Lebanon's strength,' it was then believed, 'lay in its very weakness,' and the latter forestalled its resolute involvement in regional affairs and commitment to the Arab-Israeli conflict. But isolation was untenable and the country's weakness proved to be its undoing: it eventually opened the way to its transformation into the main battlefield of the Arab-Israeli conflict. The Palestinians were the first to take advantage of the situation and, following their expulsion from Jordan in 1970, started to launch cross-border operations against Israel, triggering retaliatory raids on targets within Lebanese territory. Lebanon was dragged into an undeclared war against Israel, which exacerbated its own internal contradictions and contributed to the outbreak of a much more serious war which wrecked Lebanon for close to 15 years.

Lebanon's war started in 1975. At the outset, it revolved around two main issues: the reform of the socio-political system and the Palestinian presence.

Accordingly, two main camps emerged: the 'Christian-conservative' camp, which sought to preserve a political system that had ensured its ascendancy and to curtail the armed Palestinian presence, and the 'Islamic-progressive' camp, a motley coalition of traditional Islamic leaders and leftist parties which aimed at reforming the political system to reflect their own, divergent interests. While the traditional Islamic politicians strove to maintain the communitarian setting and to improve their own role within the system in line with the increasing demographic importance of Muslim communities, the leftist parties aimed at a more radical economic, social and political reform that would do away with a communitarian system that blocked any such progress. Both sides within the 'Islamic-progessive' camp agreed, however, on one thing: in return for their support for the Palestinian Resistance, they expected the Palestinians to advance their own local cause.

With the collapse of the Lebanese state and army in 1976, the war slipped out of the control of all sides. The initial local rationale for the war – the reform of the political system and the determination of Lebanon's foreign policy – was swiftly submerged by much higher stakes. Although Lebanese parties pursed their petty wars – which now involved new and varied actors, constant shifts in alliances and, as the war dragged on, the disintegration of all coalitions and a pointless war of all against all – they actually became mere pawns in the hands of more powerful regional and international parties. The latter included most notably the PLO, Syria, Israel, the United States and the Soviet Union. While the PLO was neutralised in 1982, and the US and the USSR contented themselves with remote supervisory roles, Syria and Israel increasingly held sway. Lebanon emerged as the proxy battlefield where they faced each other in a subtly choreographed rivalry that stopped short of direct confrontation. At the same time, to perpetuate its presence in Lebanon, Syria strove to manipulate intra-Lebanese divisions to its own advantage, supporting in turn the Christians, the Druse and the Shiites, and eventually succeeding in imposing its supremacy over all.

As a result, when the war ended in 1989 with the signing of the Taif Agreement, the Lebanese were the prime losers. Their country was devastated, all parties were exhausted but none could claim to have prevailed. The Christians had, it seemed, lost most: their ascendancy within the system was curtailed, their leadership was annihilated and they were more divided and bewildered than ever before. However, the victory of the Muslim parties was as elusive. Although they gained on paper a larger share of power and a bigger say politically, they were not allowed to exploit their newly gained prerogatives; these were largely usurped by Syria. Indeed, the architects of the Taif Agreement, in acknowledgement of Syria's strategic, political and economic interests in Lebanon, endorsed, on a temporary basis, the continued military Syrian presence with a view to helping the Lebanese government disarm the militias and establish its authority.

Following the Gulf War in 1990, and the launching of the Palestinian-Israeli peace process in 1991, with the tacit agreement of the Arab states, the United States and other western powers which sought to reward it for rallying the pro-western coalition and for joining the peace negotiations, Syria secured a free hand in Lebanon and twisted most of the terms of the Taif agreement in its favour. Syria alone emerged as the uncontested winner of the Lebanese war and the main power broker in Lebanon, controlling all political appointments, together with local, foreign and defence policy decisions.

Syria's ascendancy was again reinforced with the withdrawal of the Israeli forces from Lebanon in May this year. Paradoxically however, Syria's victory could prove less rewarding and more problematic than seems. Indeed, Israel's withdrawal has deprived Syria of its main leverage in coercing Israel into the surrender of the entire Golan Heights: namely,

Hizbullah's implacable war against Israeli forces in south Lebanon. Moreover, Syria's recent victory, followed by the death of its uncontested leader, Hafez Assad, compels its new leadership to reassess its role in Lebanon in the light of Israel's recent pull-out and of growing rumblings of discontent in Lebanon against Syria's heavy-handed control. Although Syria does not seem ready to reciprocate the Israeli pull-out or to give up its influence there, and although the Lebanese, divided and overpowered, do not yet seem ready to claim back their country and take their fate into their hands, a new phase in Lebanese-Syrian relations is about to begin. It will take time and may not happen before a comprehensive settlement of the Arab-Israeli conflict, but for better or for worse, things are about to change.

As for Lebanon, recent developments have led many to expect the end of all its woes. Such expectations are misplaced. Although the emerging regional order seems to favour a more assertive role for Lebanon, its future will mostly depend on the Lebanese themselves. Ten years after their civil war, it is time they grappled with the political, economic and social problems besetting the country. Continuing to ignore them in the hope they will go away is no solution. ❏

Carol Hakim is a writer and researcher. Her forthcoming book The origins of the Lebanese national idea *will be published by IB Tauris, London, in 2001*

Sharing power

There have been numerous attempts over the years to find a satisfactory formula for power-sharing in Lebanon. None have so far proved enduring and early efforts have been rendered redundant by changes in the country's demographic balance that has shifted in favour of the Muslims.

Post-independence

Since the adoption of the 1926 Constitution, the Lebanese political system has been based on a power-sharing formula providing, 'as a provisional measure', for a proportional and 'equitable' representation of the various religious sects in public office. The informal and unwritten National Pact of 1943 refined this formula and fixed the ratios for each group: in the Chamber of Deputies, parliamentary seats were proportionally assigned according to a 6:5 ratio in favour of the Christians; in government and civil service, the ratio was 50:50, an equal division between Christians and Muslims; the three main communities were allotted the highest posts with the president a Maronite, the prime minister a Sunni Muslim, the speaker of parliament a Shia.

Post-war

At the end of the war, the power-sharing formula was amended in line with the stipulations of the Taif agreement, elaborated by the Lebanese deputies in 1989, under the supervision of Syria, Saudi Arabia, Algeria and Morocco. The terms of the Taif agreements were embedded in a new Constitution in 1990. The new formula: confirmed the proportional distribution of seats in parliament and the public offices, once more on a 'provisional basis', pending the final abolition of political communitarianism; altered the 6:5 ratio in parliament to a 50:50 one; confirmed the former allotment of the most senior posts among the main three communities, but redistributed power within the executive authority by curtailing the supremacy of the Maronite and transferring most of his prerogatives to the Council of Ministers acting as a collegiate body. ❏

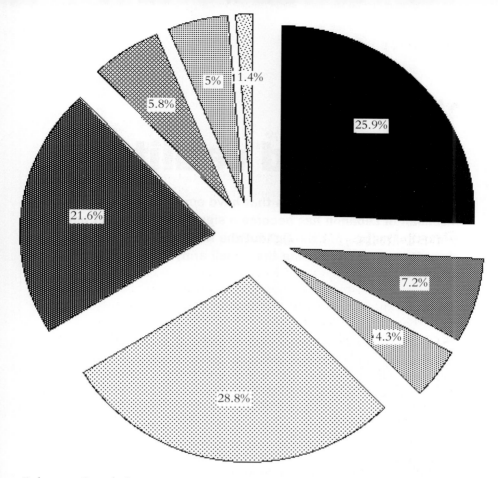

Lebanon: Population

■ Maronite (Christian) 25.9%

▨ Orthodox (Christian) 7.2%

▨ Greek Catholic (Christian) 4.3%

▨ Shi'ite (Muslim) 28.8%

▨ Sunni (Muslim) 21.6%

▨ Druze (Muslim) 5.8%

▨ Armenian (Christian: Catholics, Protestants, Orthodox) 5%

▨ Other Christian (RC, Protestant, Nestorian, Chaldean, Coptic) 1.4%

(These figures do not include non-Lebanese groups living in Lebanon including: Palestinians (325,000 – Muslim & Christian – tend to identify through nationality, not religion), Syrians & Kurds (100,000 – Muslim & Christian – Alawite, Sunnite, Orthodox, Catholic)

Source: *Lebanon: A Conflict of Minorities* Minority Rights Group © 1996

A NIZAR HAMZEH

Myth and reality

Of the many Islamist groups that have emerged within Islam, Hizbullah of Lebanon has become a significant force not only in domestic politics but throughout the Middle East, particularly since its success in driving the Israeli army from Arab land in southern Lebanon

Shi'ite aspirations for a better political and economic deal – they are Lebanon's largest sectarian group but grossly under-represented in both areas – began to take shape in the early 1970s. Under the charismatic leadership of Musa al-Sadr, founder of Amal (Hope) in 1975, the community did not adopt a militant, revivalist stance. That was left to Hizbullah (Party of God), whose militant radicalism was inspired by the Iranian revolution in 1979.

The ideological origins of Hizbullah, however, go back to Iraq rather than Iran. Iraq in the 1960s was home to a Shi'ite religio-political revival in the *hawzat al-ilmiyyah* (circles of learning) in the holy city of Najaf led by Ayatollah Muhammad Baqir al-Sadr. These circles became the epicentre of Shi'i activism and the home of Hizb al-Da'wah al-Islamiyyah (Party of Islamic Call), which sought to propagate its message throughout the Shia communities of Iraq, Iran, Lebanon and the Gulf as a prelude to revolution. Virtually all Lebanon's major Shi'i leaders came out of the Najaf *hawzat* including Ayatollah Muhammad Husayn Fadlallah, Shaykh Muhammad Mahdi Shams al-Din, Shaykh Subhi Tufayli, Sayyid Abbas al-Musawi and Sayyid Hasan Nasrallah.

Once settled in Lebanon, the shaykhs established *hawzat* under the aegis of the Da'wah Party. Yet it was not until the disappearance of Musa al-Sadr in 1978 and the victory of Iran's Islamic revolution in 1979 that the call for *jihad* (holy war) became real and a revolutionary programme based on that of Iran's Ayatollah Khomeini emerged. The Israeli invasion of June 1982 delivered a mass Shia constituency to Hizbullah for its subsequent *jihad* against Israel, the South Lebanese Army (SLA), the Lebanese forces, the rival Shia grouping Amal and the US- and French-led multinational forces. This was further strengthened with the dispatch of 1,500 Iranian Revolutionary Guards to the Syrian-controlled Beqaa region that same summer. Hizbullah was secretly formed with joint Iranian-Syrian sponsorship. For the former, it was a tangible demonstration of its intention to export the Islamic revolution; for Syria, Hizbullah was an essential instrument in its proxy war against Israel and in the preservation of its interest in Lebanon.

Hizbullah subscribes to Khomeini's theory of the governance of the *wilayat al-faqih* (religious jurist), the supreme and absolute authority at the head of a theocratic state. Long-term accommodation or compromise with Lebanon's complex confessional arrangements is, therefore, out of the question. Hizbullah's political game as an opposition force in Lebanon has more to do with 'one man, one vote, once and only once' than with a democratic conversion to parliamentary government. *Jihad* coexists with Hizbullah's parliamentary role and is called into action when the need arises. Whatever the mode at any given moment, the aim remains the same: the seizure of political power and imposition of clerical government.

Hizbullah's oscillation between militancy and political pragmatism has always been determined by a given situation. After the Israeli invasion of 1982, for instance, *jihad* against the enemies of Islam was a popular move: it targeted Israel and the SLA in the south, the US embassy and the US and French military compounds in Beirut. Hizbullah was seen as the most prominent actor in compelling Israel's retreat to their self-proclaimed security zone and prompting the withdrawal of the multi-national force from Lebanon in 1984. It was also believed to be responsible for kidnapping dozens of westerners and holding them hostage, in some cases for up to seven years.

Hizbullah's militancy also had a target closer home: its main Shia rival, Amal, now under the leadership of Nabih Berri. From 1986 to 1989, Hizbullah fought Amal for control of the Shia areas in Beirut, Beqaa and the south. It ended with Amal's defeat and Hizbullah's supremacy, particularly in the suburbs and slums on the southern outskirts of the capital where Shia fleeing the Israeli-Palestinian conflict in the south had settled.

Hizbullah's organisational structure remained largely invisible. It was led by a collective leadership composed of the seven-member *shura* (consultative) council linked directly to Khomeini with Shakh Fadlallah as its spiritual leader. Its military apparatus was backed by the Martyr's foundation and the Islamic Health Committee, both active in grass-roots social welfare work. With Tehran financing 90% of this work after 1984, Hizbullah won many recruits in the poorer Shi'a areas.

By the end of the 1980s, with Lebanon inching toward a Syrian-guaranteed peace based on the Taif Accord, Iran under President Hashemi Rafsanjani anxious to avoid confrontation with the West and Syria's determination that Islamist groups, (including its one-time protégé Hizbullah), must not expand at the cost of Lebanon's newly balanced confessional arrangement, militant activity was curtailed.

While the Islamic resistance continued its attacks against Israel in the south throughout the 1990s, Hizbullah began to evolve into a political party, more committed to grass-roots social welfare activities than to military recruitment. It runs three hospitals, over 20 medical centres and a commercial network that includes supermarkets, gas stations, department stores and construction companies. Its bid for political power within the system in the parliamentary elections of 1992 and 1996 gave it eight seats the first time, seven the second. But its real show of strength came with its success in the municipal elections of 1998 when it won almost 30 municipalities in the south, 25 in the Beqaa and two in Beirut's southern suburbs.

Since then, Hizbullah has, predictably perhaps, split along ideological lines with its former secretary general, Shaykh Subhi Tufayli, rejecting the party's political activity in favour of continuing *jihad*. His creation of a rival movement, Ansar Allah (Friends of Allah), led to his expulsion from Hizbullah in the summer of 1998.

With the liberation of the south, the likelihood of pressure from Syria restraining cross-border action against Israel, the possibility of a peace deal and Iran's rapprochement with the West, it looks increasingly difficult – if not impossible – for Hizbullah to continue its military operations. But if Hizbullah drops this aspect of its activity, settles for long-term accommodation with the system and abandons its original aims, it risks disintegration and the loss of its appeal as a party. ❑

A Nizar Hamzeh is associate professor at the American University of Beirut

AVI SHLAIM

Operation truth

**The withdrawal of the Israel Defence Force from southern
Lebanon at the end of May brought to an inglorious end Israel's
22-year-old misadventure in that country. It also marked the end
of illusions, most notably the illusion that Israel could achieve
security through the occupation of Arab land and the
employment of surrogate forces**

The collapse of Israel's self-proclaimed 'security zone' in Lebanon and
the melting away of its Christian proxy, the South Lebanon Army,
exposed in the most dramatic fashion the bankruptcy of Israel's entire
strategy for the defence of its northern border.

The 'security zone' was established in 1978 as a buffer between the
Palestinian guerrillas and Israel. In 1982, the right-wing Likud
government headed by Menachem Begin launched the ill-conceived and
ill-starred invasion of Lebanon, officially named 'Operation Peace for
Galilee'. The real purpose of the war, however, was not to achieve peace
but to impose Israeli hegemony over the entire Levant by destroying the
PLO military infrastructure in southern Lebanon, expelling the Syrian
forces from the country, and helping Israel's Maronite allies to forge a
new political order in Lebanon.

The real driving force behind the invasion of Lebanon was the
minister of defence, Ariel Sharon, and his aims were even more
ambitious and far-reaching. He developed what came to be known as
the 'big plan': the use of Israel's military power to make it the dominant
power in the Middle East. In Sharon's big plan, the war in Lebanon was
intended to transform the situation not only in Lebanon, but in the
entire region. The destruction of the PLO, he reasoned, would break the
backbone of Palestinian nationalism and facilitate the absorption of the
West Bank into Greater Israel. The resulting influx of Palestinians from

Lebanon and the West Bank into Jordan would eventually sweep away the Hashemite monarchy and transform the East Bank into a Palestinian state. And Jordan's conversion into a Palestinian state would end international pressures on Israel to withdraw from the West Bank.

None of these far-reaching aims was achieved by the invasion of Lebanon. Moreover, the war shattered the myth that all Israel's wars are defensive wars, wars of *ein breira*, of no choice. Israel's previous wars, with the exception of the 1956 Suez War, had been imposed by the Arabs. Even the Suez War commanded a broad national consensus because it was seen as a legitimate response to Arab provocation, was short, and did not involve high casualties. The war in Lebanon, on the other hand, by Menachem Begin's own admission, was 'a war of choice'. The war path was deliberately chosen by its leaders in pursuit of power and some highly controversial political and strategic gains.

What the war did do was to give birth to Hizbullah. Following the evacuation of Yasser Arafat's Palestinian fighters to Tunis in August 1982, a small, indigenous Islamic guerrilla force emerged to continue the fight against the 'Zionist enemy' with the help of Syria and Iran. Israel's large and clumsy army was no match for this small but disciplined, dedicated, and increasingly daring guerrilla force. As Israel's casualties mounted, its troops in Lebanon became demoralised, and public pressure to bring the boys back home intensified.

The withdrawal from Lebanon had been greeted with a sigh of relief by most Israelis, but there was also a general awareness that Israel was forced to retreat from Lebanon with its tail between its legs. There was no disguising the fact that the once legendary IDF had been defeated by a tiny Islamic guerrilla force. The psychological wounds left by this humiliating defeat will take a long time to heal. And humiliation is compounded by the fear that other Islamic resistance movements in the occupied territories, such as Hamas and Islamic Jihad, might resort to the same tactics that had proved so effective in driving the IDF out of Lebanon.

If one problem with the Israeli withdrawal from Lebanon was that it left implacable enemies behind, another problem was that it was not part of a regional settlement. There has always been a linkage between Israel's relations with Lebanon and Israel's relations with Syria. A major reason for the persistence of the Israeli occupation of south Lebanon despite its failure to produce security was the expectation of a broader settlement with Syria. The Israeli hope was that in return for withdrawal from the Golan Heights they would get not only peace with Syria but a Syrian guarantee of the security of their northern border. But the diplomatic deadlock on the Syrian front meant that Syria had no incentive to keep Hizbullah on a short leash. On the contrary, Syria sought to preserve its militant Islamic allies as well as small groups of Palestinian rejectionists in order to drive home the message that there could be no peace on Israel's northern border without the approval of Damascus.

At the time of withdrawal, the world's attention naturally focused on Israel. Little attention was paid to the consequences of the Israeli withdrawal for Lebanon itself. Yet the Lebanese are the real victims of Israel's prolonged misadventure across its northern border. In a broader sense, Lebanon is victim of the cruel geopolitics of the region, with two aggressive and overbearing neighbours in the shape of Israel and Syria.

The names chosen by Israel for its repeated violations of Lebanon's sovereignty carry more than a trace of self-righteousness: Operation Peace for Galilee, Operation Accountability and Operation Grapes of Wrath. It is high time Israel accounted for the sustained suffering to which it has subjected the civilian population of southern Lebanon over the last two decades. Its withdrawal might well be named Operation Moment of Truth.

Israelis, too, have paid a heavy price for the megalomania and mistakes of their right-wing leaders. Nearly 1,000 Israeli soldiers have lost their lives in Lebanon and the lives of their families have been blighted. A poignant example is Yacov Guterman whose only son Raz was killed on the first night of the Lebanon war in the battle for Beaufort Castle. The bereaved father sent an open letter to the three principal architects of the Lebanon war: Menachem Begin, the prime minister; Ariel Sharon, the defence minister; and Rafael Eytan, the chief of staff. The letter, which was published in the daily newspaper *Ha'aretz* on 5 July 1982, condemned their wickedness for starting a cynical and superfluous war, a war whose motives were purely political and nationalist. Guterman accused them of dark chauvinism and blind adventurism. He protested that they were sacrificing Israel's innocent boys in a war of deceit and described their pointless death as murder. The letter ended with the following words:

> 'If you still have a spark of conscience and humanity within you,
> my great pain – the suffering of a father in Israel whose entire

Debris of war in south Lebanon – Credit: Norbert Schiller

world has been destroyed – will haunt you, even in your sleep. Day and night, wherever you are, and for the rest of time, your forehead will bear the mark of Cain.'

On 2 June 2000, soon after Israel's prolonged and purposeless presence in southern Lebanon came to an end, Yacov Guterman published another article in *Ha'aretz*. Any civilized nation, he observed, would move to punish the politicians who had brought such tragedy upon it. In Israel, however, the architects of the Lebanon war had not been called to account. It was shocking to find, for example, that Ariel Sharon, the evil spirit behind the war, had been elected to the leadership of the Likud. Such is the man's insensitivity and shamelessness, exclaimed Guterman, that he takes every opportunity to offer advice based on his 'expertise' on Lebanon. There was something that

Guterman wanted to tell those wretched creatures after the most terrible 18 years of his life:

> 'On your knees, on your knees all you liars who talked about "40km", who deluded us with "40 years of calm for Israel", on your knees all you fraudsters who talked about "the threat to Israel's existence". Repent, all you evil nationalists, you who, instead of striving with all your might for a political compromise that would hold for generations, callously sent whole units into fire and death.
>
> As soon as the last of our soldiers had left Lebanon, you should have hurried to Israel's military cemeteries. There, you should have fallen on your knees, dressed in sackcloth and ashes, as was Israel's ancient custom. There, you should have torn out your hair and begged forgiveness from all those murdered young men of Israel, men whose innocence and love of their country you exploited so shamelessly.'

Guterman noted with bitterness that not one of the right-wing leaders sunk to his knees, and that not one of them put on sackcloth and ashes. Not one of them took the slightest responsibility for what happened, and none has yet been judged.

Yet Guterman believes that the nation has learned a lesson, and in the hardest and most painful way. He thinks that in the future the people might beware, as of fire, of the 'violent nationalism which at all times in history has wrapped itself in the mantle of a patriotism claiming to act 'for the good of the "nation". And always, too, leaves behind nothing but ruins, destruction, blood and tears.' One can only hope that Yacov Guterman is right and that the Israeli public has learned its lesson. For it has been, in Rudyard Kipling's words, no end of a lesson. ❏

Avi Shlaim *is a fellow of St Antony's College and a professor of International Relations at the University of Oxford. He is author of* War and Peace in the Middle East *(1995), and* The Iron Wall: Israel and the Arabs *(2000)*

ZIYAD MAKHOUL

Shit house

The 'right of return' is not high on the present Israeli-Palestinian peace agenda. But in camps like Beirut's Sabra and Shatila, refugees from wars as long ago as 1948 continue to hold out hope...

The first shock on arrival at the camp is the vast wasteland of rubbish. It stretches in every direction as far as the eye can see. Hordes of flies, dozens of kids, dirty, shoeless teenagers hover over the rubble. No one seems overly concerned; everywhere children spill out on to the streets – the schools are closed. We rejoin our guides, Amine and Fathi, who immediately begin to unburden themselves of the many problems and pains that are part of daily life here. We go into a house fabricated from metal sheeting. The stench from the urine-soaked mattress is overpowering. We say hello, gagging; the smell is suffocating, inhuman; and the flies are everywhere.

Abu-Saleh sits among his family, nine of them in the one room scarcely ten metres square. He can't move around these days: his right foot is rotting away with gangrene. 'It's diabetes. UNRWA [United Nations Relief and Works Agency, created in 1949 to deal with Palestinian refugees] won't do anything for me and I don't have the money for surgery, or for medicine, or for the hospital. They just give me aspirin.'

We move on to the first of the cemeteries. It runs alongside the heavily rutted road, up to the football ground where the kids are kicking cans around. The sea is a little further. The beach used to be a paradise, so what's gone wrong now? 'The trash comes down this way and empties into the sea; all the refuse and filth, all the miseries of humanity: the sum of our sorrows. Of course it's grey. What do you expect? How could it be anything else.'

September 1982, Israeli-backed Phalangist militia massacred between 600 and 2000 people in Sabra and Shatila camps – Credit: Rex Features

The schools are in a state of decay. 'There is no organised programme, no staff replacements and UNRWA is economising: they hire teachers barely 20 years old with virtually no training.' Amine and Fathi let rip on corruption: the misappropriation of funds, the way their 'countrymen' line their pockets, 'even now, when there isn't even enough to go round'. 'Yes, that's the benefits office. It doles out the food, the rations that keep us going. We get flour that's past its sell-by date, milk when there is any, chickpeas and, for the very poorest who have next to nothing to live on, there is US$10 every three months from UNRWA.'

Amine and Fathi talk about kids who spend the whole day drugged out of their minds; about incest and people who go down to Beirut to gather empty cans for recyling which they then sell for a derisory amount. There are children killing time by filling a small wheelbarrow with garbage and then emptying it on the graves in the second cemetery, slap in the middle of the camp. 'Every time someone dies, we have to open up the graves and rearrange everything; there are five or six bodies in every grave,' people tell us. 'Like that young man they've just buried. He did six years as a student in Moscow and then got assassinated by the Russian mafia. His family had to wait 40 days for the body to be returned.'

'I dream of a Jordanian-Palestinian federation where most of my fellow Palestinian refugees from Lebanon can go and settle,' says Juliette, a young Palestinian studying at Beirut University. 'They can't stay here; the Lebanese don't want them.' Juliette bridles as she speaks, like any other young Palestinian, as she remembers her father promising her when she was small that, 'we shall return to Jaffa and eat the best oranges in the world'. Juliette smiles wickedly as she mentions her two grandmothers, the one Jewish and the other Caucasian; and her Lebanese mother and Palestinian father. ❏

Ziyad Makhoul *is a journalist with Beirut's* L'Orient-le jour *in which this article first appeared.*
Translated by JVH

SAMIR KASSIR

Red lines and media blues

It's a long way back to the 'oasis of freedom' in which the Lebanese media once luxuriated

In an article written shortly after President Hafez Assad's death, the Syrian dissident Riad Turk spoke of his country as a 'kingdom of fear'. The description does not apply to Syrian-controlled Lebanon and will probably never do so. Yet Lebanon no longer qualifies as the 'oasis of freedom' of the Middle East that its political mythology has repeatedly claimed. Instead, it has entered an era of limited freedom where what remains of public liberties are being progressively curtailed in the interests of those in power – or those that pull their strings.

You could say Lebanon is retreating on itself, not only in terms of its own history, but also compared with developments in other Arab countries over the last two decades. Though social behaviour remains more liberal in Lebanon than in any other Arab society, political and civil liberties are similar to those under the Mexican-style democracies in Egypt, Morocco and Jordan. In all these countries, substantial steps towards freedom of speech failed to foster a substantial shift in the structure of political and economic power.

Given the state of official dealings with the media, current trends could lead to further deterioration, even to the restriction of public expression as demonstrated by several recent cases of censorship: against Marcel Khalifé for singing a poem citing a verse from the Quran; against the Maurice Béjart dance company for wearing improper clothes in a ballet dedicated to the late Arab diva Oum Koulthoum; against the non-political foreign press for publishing allegedly 'immoral' photographs and advertisements; and against numerous books for supposedly violating religious or sexual taboos.

Beirut streets during and after the war – Credit: Norbert Schiller

Although the Syrian regime has never refrained from coercion in Lebanon, including political assassination, it has shown a marked preference for avoiding such practices as long as its control is not fundamentally challenged. And while it has managed to manipulate the political institutions of the Lebanese Republic, Syria has also learned how to deal with a pluralistic media and even to use such pluralism to its own advantage.

★★★

Freedom of speech is in principle guaranteed by the Constitution, both in its original version of 1926 and in its amended form after the Taif agreement of 1989. The laws governing publishing and broadcasting do not demand prior censorship for locally published books and media products. Two years ago, a law authorising prior censorship of Lebanese newspapers – adopted in the late 1970s but not used except for one year – was abrogated. The press is only subject to judicial control, under the provisions of a relatively liberal law, except for the prohibition of criticism against foreign heads of states and the so-called 'instigation of confessional rivalries'. The same general provisions apply to news broadcasting.

But such a liberal vision stops, literally, at the borders: to cross these borders allows the General Security Directorate to intervene. It is not only the import of books, newspapers, magazines and movies, including advertisements, that is subject to censorship, but also their export. Publishing houses need an export licence from the General Security Directorate for each title they want to send abroad. If such a provision tends to prevent criticism against other Arab countries – and the ensuing retaliation it could provoke from these countries – it also helps to keep publishers under permanent scrutiny and allows hasty judicial steps when it becomes necessary to ban a book. Needless to say, this procedure, especially when strictly operated as it is under President Lahoud and General Jamil Sayyid, director-general of general security, inhibits the development of joint ventures with the international publishing industry, depriving the country of substantial incomes.

Another limit to freedom is the licence system governing the publication of newspapers, magazines, books and broadcasting. It is unconstitutional and contrary to the UN Chart of Human Rights; but it does help government control over the industry. That is so far as non-political publications are concerned. When it comes to political newspapers and magazines, the licence system is an obstacle to the development of a truly free press. Under the current system, based on a biased interpretation of obsolete laws, any new venture needs to borrow a licence costing from US$350,000 to US$500,000 dollars, depending on supply and demand. Needless to say, such a prerequisite largely prevents the creation of new publications.

Nor does the scale of the Lebanese market help with investment. Already tiny before the war, readership has shrunk dramatically as a result of competition from television, the depoliticisation of society and, probably, a drop in professional standards. The total readership of all Lebanese dailies today amounts to no more than a few tens of thousands, less than the readership of a single paper in 1975. Newspapers can no longer live off their earnings and are heavily dependent on advertising, a sector that has already displayed its hostility to media innovation and political engagement. The monopoly enjoyed by one man, Antoine Choueri, in the advertising world, not only discourages innovation in the press, it also facilitates official pressures, as was underlined by the political and financial onslaught against the Lebanese Broadcasting Corporation (LBC) two years ago.

The lack of commercial viability keeps the Lebanese press under the control of political money, not known to favour a change in the status quo, even when it opposes the government. The archetype of political money, the billionaire and former prime minister, Rafiq Hariri, enjoyed substantial influence in the media world, both as an official shareholder and as a result of his willingness to submit to blackmail by various papers.

Yet the main restrictions on the freedom of the press in post-war Lebanon have nothing to do with the legal framework nor the economic structure of the media and publishing industries. Informal weapons are more powerful: the intimidation and manipulation of journalists and publishers determine the news agenda. Journalists learn to avoid certain subjects or resort to a form of 'code' based on understatement and allusion to avoid crossing the tacit 'red lines'. Practical experience makes it clear that the lines are subject to change or, more accurately, displacement that can widen the area of public discussion. If what Lebanese journalists and intellectuals call 'raising the ceiling' (*raf' al-saqf*) has been possible in the past decade, it was not in any way because of a green light from Lebanese or Syrian authorities, but the result of a gradual reclaiming of free speech: a continuous process of trial and error pursued by a bunch of journalists acting slowly – since the 'error' in such a process could be lethal – but steadily to improve their own freedom.

As a result, and especially after 1995, many issues journalists would go out of their way to avoid, including those related to Syrian tutelage over Lebanon, have entered public debate. Even the term 'Syrian occupation' is used, even though it is not strictly accurate. Indeed, what remained of the red lines were more to do with the nature of the Syrian regime and its sectarian character than with Syrian policy in Lebanon. Words like 'dictator' or 'dictatorship' are avoided as well as any disrespectful reference to the late president or his family, but even this last taboo began to vanish in the last weeks of Assad's life.

Strangely, improvements in the coverage of Syrian–Lebanese issues have been counterbalanced by a clear regression in the discussion of domestic matters since the appointment of General Emile Lahoud as head of state in 1998. Under President Elias Hrawi (1989-1998) and Rafiq Hariri's tenure as prime minister (1992-1998), public criticism of Lebanese officials became increasingly vocal. Splits among the ruling elite and the ensuing trading of accusations and insults between Syria's assorted clients, gave the press greater leeway for its criticisms. But with the election of Lahoud to the presidency, Lahoud's person and policy became a no-go area. Featuring the president in cartoons was informally but effectively prohibited and still is; a cult of personality was stage-managed by his security services. But as the economy deteriorated and the public administration sank into paralysis, the image cracked and criticism crept closer and closer to the presidential person – though it does not yet fully reflect the general derision in which he is held. The candidacy of his 25-year-old son in this year's elections, gave journalists their first real opportunity to criticise his tenure. The ill-management of the electoral campaign by the security apparatus gave journalists licence to attack yet another sacred cow. Official propaganda in the form of state TV and street decorations, continues to offer the image of a heroic president.

While Lebanon's press cannot be called free, there are still independent journalists, the International Federation of Human Rights commented recently. The real problem is in radio and TV where journalists are given very little room for manoeuvre, and where the allocation of broadcasting licences mirrors the distribution of power among Syria's clients.

After a post-war de facto deregulation that can only be compared to the proliferation of private television stations in early-1980s Italy, a 1997 law organising the industry reduced the number of networks to seven, including state-owned Télé-Liban and Hizbullah's Al-Manar – the latter was authorised to operate without a licence on a temporary basis to provide a voice for the armed resistance against Israeli occupation. Four licences were granted on a permanent basis with the proviso that the terms of references be strictly observed. Unsurprisingly, they were shared out among key political figures and reflect the country's confessional power balance: Future Television to the then prime minister, Hariri; Murr TV to the interior minister's brother – today at odds with his benefactor; National Broadcasting Network to the parliamentary speaker Nabih Berri; and the older Lebanese Broadcasting Corporation to Suleiman Franjieh, a government minister and prime Christian client of the Assad family. To counterbalance Al-Manar, the Christians were allowed to start up their own channel, Télé-Lumière.

In the name of coherence, all the above networks were allowed to operate a sister radio station. Two or three independent stations were also authorised. Needless to say, the legal provision limiting individual equity to ten per cent remained a fiction, as did the provision forbidding cross ownership. In both cases, the Levantine extended family came in handy, but for most 'investors', as for their Syrian mentor, their interest in the media has little to do with profits and everything to do with power, influence and public exposure.

Yet despite the restrictions ownership of the channels imposes, there are journalists, even in LBC, who manage to do a decent job: one of LBC's political and cultural talk shows consistently gets the top ratings in Arab satellite channels. But this success, like others elsewhere, is totally dependent on individual journalists' willingness to pay the price of maintaining professional standards and personal conscience. There is no professional body to protect them, media owners are unwilling to defend their own freedom and they have no recourse against arbitrary dismissal. But they do it; and this is the brighter side of a bleak picture. ❏

Samir Kassir *is a senior columnist with* An-Nahar *daily and a contributor to*

SAMIR KASSIR

Le Monde Diplomatique. *His most recent book is* La Guerre du Liban: de la dissension nationale au conflit regional (From national dispute to regional conflict) *Karthala, Paris (1994)*

Its master's voice

The history of the Lebanese Broadcasting Corporation makes an interesting case study of the way these things are managed in Lebanon

Launched in 1985 at the height of the civil war by the Lebanese Forces, the main Christian militia, LBC quickly succeeded in reaching a nationwide audience, far beyond its natural political constituency. Its position remained unchallenged even after the war and the proliferation of new channels. Even the dismantling of the Lebanese Forces and the dramatic fall of their chief, Samir Geagea, in 1994, failed to affect its commanding position.

Finally faced with the threat of closure as a result of Syrian mistrust and Hariri's personal interests in Future Television, general manager Pierre Daher reconstituted the old LBC in a new company, LBCI (I for international), in which he took a majority shareholding, dividing the remainder among close business associates. He then put himself and his company under the political protection of Suleiman Franjieh, Geagea's arch-rival, a minister in Hariri's government and a cherished Syrian ally. The restructuring of the company and the entry of his close ally, the billionaire and eventual MP Issam Fares, as a shareholder, gave Franjieh substantial equity.

Having ensured LBC's survival and gained a new political patron, Daher, who was by then chairman, consolidated his position by securing partnerships with Saudi investors after developing LBC's satellite channels and creating a series of off-shore companies. By now, he was nurturing political ambitions and playing the opposition against Hariri, an echo of his master Franjieh's voice; a folly for which he was soon to pay the price. Twice.

After failing to get Syrian endorsement of his candidacy in the 1996 elections, Daher forced a showdown with Hariri in early 1998 by airing an interview with one of the prime minister's fiercest opponents on LBC's satellite channel. Franjieh, however, capitulated in the face of a cabinet decision forbidding news and political programmes on all Lebanese satellite channels, namely LBC and Future.

The decision was later overruled, but LBC's political problems were not over. In mid-1998, and in the wake of a series of arrests among former members of the disbanded Lebanese Forces, Daher was subjected to a period of police and judicial harassment that lasted just as long as it took him to agree to give up his majority shareholding in LBC by 'selling' 2.5% to a Franjieh associate. Franjieh, acting on Syrian instructions, also deprived Daher of his control over the news agenda. It was handed to a former comrade in the Lebanese Forces, who rapidly transformed it into little more than a relay station for Syrian intelligence.

The channel once founded by Syria's arch-enemies has lost its critical powers. Even guests on talk shows – if they are Lebanese, Arab, Palestinian or Syrian, and especially the last two, regardless of any official position – must be approved by Damascus. But as for everyone, there was worse to come under Lahoud. Though not quite as shameless as the bulletins on state-run Télé-Liban, LBC news bears the hallmark of a security officer more clearly than any other station; it carries straight propaganda for Lahoud and scrupulously avoids giving airtime to his opponents – except, of course, when it comes to Franjieh. ❏

SK

Once upon a time...

The camera came early to the Middle East in the 1850s, along with Europeans hot foot to be the first to capture on film a set of images of its celebrated biblical and classical sites. Since then, there has been a continuous and distinguished local photographic tradition alongside that produced by the ever increasing flow of professionals and tourists. With the introduction of the Kodak box camera in the 1880s, photography became accessible to the masses and, as WWI dawned, the Middle East was rivalling western Europe as the world's photographic centre.

Set up in 1997 to gather this rich, untapped heritage, the Arab Image Foundation (AIF) has since accumulated over 25,000 photographs spanning the century between 1860 and 1970. Unique in the Arab world, the archive has photo collections, studio portraits and family albums that chronicle the social evolution of the entire Arab world. The AIF collection contains prints by prominent international photographers, such as Van Leo, as well as pictures taken by local photographers and many snapshots by 'anon'. Many have been donated by the photographers and their families, but the bulk have been rescued from the once whirring but now derelict studios of Beirut, Cairo and Jerusalem.

The collection portrays a Lebanon lost to the passage of time, but is particularly poignant in its record of a city before war dismantled it, and when Beirut was just a pleasant cosmopolitan city and people led normal, trivial lives. ❏

Lebanon 1920s: Gergess Bou Zeid, resplendent in his finery and bristling with ammunition, down from the mountains for a studio portrait in Beirut – Credit: Camille el Kareh

Lebanon 1920: Selim el Khoury and friends on a hunting trip – Credit: Anon

1931, Elias el Helou and son display the morning's catch in front of the family shop – Credit: Anon

Beirut harbour 1930: when Beirut was the mecca of the European tourist trade – Credit: Jibrail Jabbur

1943, as the battle for North Africa rages across the Mediterranean, the Bicharate family catch the mood in the studio tank — Credit: Anon

Beyrouth –
Damas.

Chemin de Fer du Liban

1929, women gather to mourn a family member – Credit: Camille el Kareh

1930, travel of a different kind. Albert Khayat with friend peers from the trans-Arabian studio express – Credit: Jules Lind

1958, the children of Amin Salam play at soldiers in a derelict building during the revolution in Beirut. Twenty-five years later, this generation found itself in the front line as full-scale fighting erupted across Beirut's 'green line' – Credit: Anon

1967, Palestinian fedayin. Driven out of Israel in 1948 and 1967, and from Jordan in 1970, camps like Sabra and Shatila became the home of numbers of Palestinian refugees and resistance fighters. The latter, like these two posing for a studio portrait to send home, were again moved on when Arafat was expelled from Beirut in 1982 – Credit: Hashem Madani

CHIBLI MALLAT

Trouble with the neighbours

For much of its modern history, Lebanon's fate has been in the hands of its neighbours. The recent election results – a rejection of Syrian control – suggests the population wants to take charge of its own destiny

The first recognisable constitutional structure of Lebanon, the *mutasarriffiyye* in Mount Lebanon, was created in 1861. It owed its existence to an agreement between the European powers and the waning Ottoman Empire. After WWI, Lebanon emerged as a French colony, part of the French–British division of the colonial spoils in the Levant. In 1943, it owed its rapid, almost painless independence to the collapse of French rule in the Levant at the time of the Nazi occupation of France. While external events might have have been less influential between 1943 and 1975, the collapse of the state during the civil war (1975-1989) allowed regional factors in the shape of the Arab-Israeli conflict, plus the second Gulf War, to play a dominant role once more. The Taif agreement of 1989 that ended the civil war fits into this pattern. Taif redefined the constitutional balance of power in the community-based system, but its implementation was subject to differing interpretations, and key domestic and regional measures were ignored.

A decade on, nothing much has changed: regional and international powers continue to assert their influence. Despite the withdrawal of Israel and the subsequent collapse of the South Lebanese Army (SLA) in May this year, the US continues to play a role. However, it is the influence of Syria that has been most significant with the lack of freedom and political representation common in Damascus gradually being mirrored in Beirut.

Lebanon has long prided itself on its respect for free expression. While the room for manoeuvre is still wider than in most Arab countries, it is narrower than at any time since independence. True, there are no acknowledged prisoners of conscience, the government has licensed a regional office of Amnesty International and the Beirut press remains the boldest in the Arab world. Email, now accessible to most educated Lebanese, delivers a wealth of information from around the world almost instantaneously; a wide array of institutions of education and public outlets in several languages keeps Lebanon at the forefront of multiculturalism. Local television, however, has been outstripped in free expression by independent satellite broadcasters in the Gulf.

But censorship has tightened, a number of former political figures remain *persona non grata* in the country and tolerance for the criticism of public figures is lower than at any time in recent years. Raymond Eddé, a leading political figure since independence, was forced into exile where he died this year. This epitomises the difficulties encountered by leaders who are not prepared to toe the line imposed by the regional powers.

There are two main constraints on free expression: the self-censorship that curtails any criticism of the president or his counterparts in the Arab world; and traditional curbs on dissent and protest. Censors prevent books from being shipped in and distributed, other works of cultural expression are subject to the censor's scissors. Harsh punishments, including beating and imprisonment, are often meted out to student protests, though protestors seldom remain in prison for long. The judiciary is constrained by its fragmented nature, a characteristic that has allowed military tribunals to dominate the judicial process as happened recently with the trials of former members of the South Lebanese Army.

As a result, the most trenchant criticism of government has appeared in circles that are not directly political, specifically among Christian religious and educational institutions, the leaders of which are relatively sheltered by the institutions they head. The rest of society is more circumspect; serious dissent is left to expatriate Lebanese.

The fetters on free expression affect the outcome of elections. Lebanon has held several elections over the past decade at municipal, parliamentary and presidential levels: parliamentary in 1992 and 1996; in 1995 and 1998, in accordance with the constitution, parliament elected a new president. In all four cases, Syrian influence was paramount.

Constitutionally, the democratic credentials of the election of the president leave a lot to be desired: it is not on the basis of universal suffrage and is further compromised by the requirement that the candidate be a Maronite Christian. In 1995 and 1998, the normal constitutional process was short-circuited by special amendments tailored, in the first instance to ensure that Elias Hrawi's mandate was extended for three years and, in the second, to ensure that General Emile Lahoud secured the presidency unopposed, despite being barred by his position in the army. In both cases, voices of dissent were few and far between and there were no serious challengers to Syria's candidate.

Parliamentary elections are a different matter, constitutionally circumscribed by the proportional allocation of seats to the religious communities – with the exclusion of some groups altogether. Other factors, many of them common to the third world, influence results: the dominance of money, rampant political and family patronage, the prior 'fixing' of electoral lists, bussing in supporters, gerrymandering of all kins and poor practical arrangements for the protection of voters. As a result, the results of the 1996 parliamentary election were less credible than the municipal elections of the same year.

The limits on free expression together with those on political representation have curtailed public debate and hindered the process of reconciliation between the various communities. Suspicion between religious groups remains well entrenched and no national programme or party crossing the sectarian boundaries has emerged. In May 2000, a further 6,000–7,000 people were displaced from south Lebanon, in the wake of the collapse of the SLA. Given their known association with Israel, the prospects for their return are remote. In the absence of reliable statisitics, the scale of emigration is uncertain, but pointers indicate a serious increase, especially among the young. While the present economic crisis is no help in stemming the exodus, its most disturbing aspect is the manifest disenchantment of youth in the face of a loss of basic freedoms and the impoverishment of the political process: more specifically, the lack of real national leadership and a mistrust even of the democratic freedom available to express one's choice. While hopes are pinned on regional relaxation following a breakthrough in Syrian-Israeli negotiations, the prospects of Lebanon's return to a vibrant democratic tradition remain uncertain. ❏

Chibli Mallat is *Professor of Law at the University of St Joseph, Beirut*

ALAIN GRESH

The road from Damascus

Doctor Bashar's had an easy start, but there's plenty of hurdles ahead

In a matter of weeks following the death of his father in June this year, 'Doctor Bashar' rose from colonel in the army and president of the society for information science to general, commander-in-chief of the armed forces, secretary-general of the Baath party and sole candidate for the presidential election in July. The whole thing was so slick it could have been dreamed up and executed by his father Hafez Assad, the man who had ruled Syria for 30 years.

Bashar, had been summoned back from London — where he was studying ophthalmology — on the sudden death of his elder brother in 1994 to be groomed as heir apparent. Despite an initial reluctance, he spent the following six years patiently building his power base in Damascus, removing anyone who expressed the slightest reservation to his programmed rise to power. He also surrounded himself with a tightly-knit guard, based on loyalty to his father, Alawite solidarity and unconditional support for his claims.

He cut his diplomatic teeth in Lebanon, where tens of thousands of Syrian soldiers were posted and at a time when conflict was raging with Israel in the south. From the spring of 1995, he gradually marginalised Vice-President Abdel Halim Khaddam, insisting that he alone handle the incessant demands for arbitration coming from the south. His influence was apparent in the election of General Emile Lahoud to the Lebanese presidency in October 1998 and the resignation of Prime Minister Rafiq Hariri in the same year.

In 1999, he made his appearance on the regional scene with an official visit to Jordan in February. That summer he was in Saudi Arabia,

Kuwait, Bahrain and Oman. He met the Iranian president, Mohammad Khatami, when he visited Damascus in October, and is due to return the visit to Syria's strategic ally soon. He made his debut on the international scene. In November, he made his first official trip outside the Arab world, to France where he met President Jacques Chirac – with whom Ehud Barak was already discussing the Syrian side of the peace process. A few weeks later, Syrian-Israeli talks were under way after being blocked for almost four years.

But it is the army and the intelligence services who hold the reins of power in Damascus. He made use of a crash course at officer's college to establish his first network among the young officers who, together with the technocrats close to him, form what is called the Bashar generation. In an interview with the weekly *Al Wasat* last August, Bashar criticised the 'old guard': 'They are people of a certain generation who have amassed profits and power which they're guarding jealously. They don't want to allow anyone near.' While he admits there are those who 'have won major victories for the public good', it is safe to predict that some of the regime's grandees who harbour reservations about the dynastic succession will face retirement and corruption charges.

By 1996, Bashar had sorted out his troublesome cousins who were causing trouble in Latakia and the Alawite hinterland; three years later, he saw off his ambitious uncle Rifaat for the last time in a pitched battle that brought the region of Rifaat's old fiefdoms under his control. Meanwhile, he strengthened his control over the security services, in particular the most powerful of them, military intelligence, the head of which, General Ali Duba, was forced to retire this February and was replaced by General Hassan Khalil, considered a second-ranking figure, leaving one of Bashar's followers, Assef Shawkat, as the real strongman.

Retirement helped him get rid of other offenders. In summer 1998, the Sunni army chief, Hikmat Shehabi, was replaced by his Alawite deputy, General Ali Aslan. Then, in June last year, the air-force chief, Muhammad Khouli, and a number of other officers were also removed from office. However, some members of the old guard, like the defence minister, Mustafa Tlas, and General Aslan had their appointments prolonged past the fateful age. The point was not age but loyalty.

In barely five years Bashar had formed a protective phalanx around himself. Along with the Bashar generation, it has members of the old guard like Tlas and Aslan, and also people from the generation between

– now in its 50s – like Shawkat and General Bahjat Suleiman, who was made head of internal security in 1999.

Bashar also knew how to play to the populace. With his technical background, he knew how to cultivate his image as a moderniser and he was not afraid to attack privilege and corruption. In September 1998, to general stupefaction, bulldozers demolished villas that had been built illegally by high-ranking Alawites. A few weeks earlier, General Bashir al-Najjar, head of state security, had been arrested and sentenced to 12 years' imprisonment.

The new, younger government formed this spring under Mustafa Miro quickened the pace of the fight against corruption. Mahmud Zoubi, prime minster for almost 13 years, was expelled from the party on 10 May. He committed suicide on 21 May. In the days leading up to the announcement of Assad's death, accusations were directed at General Shehabi, army chief of staff for 24 years and one of the symbols of the regime. Apparently well-informed sources in Damascus announced that he was to be charged with corruption, in particular, of having covered up for Zoubi. Shehabi abruptly left Beirut, where he was having treatment, and flew to the US. The press reported that Rafiq Hariri, former Lebanese prime minister, and Vice-President Khaddam saw him off. On 8 June, a report from Damascus in *Al Hayat* commented : 'No one is above the law'. And sources close to Bashar added that corruption was 'the same everywhere' and that the corrupt 'were ganging up together'.

Two days later came the announcement of Assad's death. Khaddam, first vice-president, who was in principle in charge in the interim, did no more than sign decrees preparing a reform to the constitution, lowering the age for election to the presidency to 34, and the promotion of Bashar to the rank of general and the post of army chief of staff. Thereafter, Bashar, and Bashar alone, would have real power. He masterminded his father's funeral, during which he accepted the allegiance of all the authorities. He actively prepared the Baath Party congress which took place on the appointed dates, between 17 and 21 June, where he was elected secretary-general of the party, introduced several of his close supporters, in particular Mustafa Miro, the prime minister, Farouk al-Sharaa, the foreign minister, and Ghiyat Barakat, an Internet specialist from Aleppo, to membership, and increased the number of military in the party. Shehabi was removed from the regional command, and Duba and Khouli were replaced by, among others, the heads of the four main intelligence agencies, Ali Aslan, chief of staff of the armed forces, and his deputies, and the commander of Syrian troops in Lebanon, General Ibrahim al-Safi. Maher al-Assad, Bashar's younger brother and an officer in the Republican Guard, and another of its officers, Manaf Tlas, son of the defence minister, also joined the committee.

For the time being, Bashar has ensured the cohesion of his minority Alawite community, and intends to reinforce the regime's alliance with the Sunni bourgeoisie who make up two-thirds of the population as against the Alawites' ten per cent. But he must also ensure that the expectations of the younger generation who see in him the beginning of a new and better life are met, and the profound economic and social problems of the country tackled.

There are also numerous challenges outside the country. Like the elusive peace with Israel. He may have said he is ready to go down that path, but he has also reiterated his father's preconditions: the withdrawal of Israeli troops to the 4 June 1967 borders.

And then there is Lebanon. It's difficult to see exactly what the consequences of the Syrian transition will be, but there's no doubt things will change; as, indeed, the victory of several candidates contesting the August/Sepember elections on an anti-Syrian platform, have already demonstrated. In the first place, the is the removal of the 'Hafez' factor: for 30 years, the name alone was enough to instil fear and dread into his population. Lebanese as well as Syrians internalised the sense of his all-powerful presence. His death is not going to cause a major upheaval, but the game has already changed: people are more willing to say what they think, for instance.

More than that: if President Bashar is really going to get down to the modernisation and renewal of Syria, he cannot allow the status quo to persist in Lebanon. For domestic reasons, he needs Lebanon prosperous, an extra 'lung' for his economic reforms back home. The Israeli retreat from the south of Lebanon also means he has to change tactics in Lebanon if he doesn't want to be assailed by the international community calling for reciprocal withdrawal by Syrian troops. Interestingly, the US never demanded such a withdrawal even during the Israli-Syrian peace negotiations. However, it is a factor that weighs in the scales of change. For Damascus, Lebanon is an important card in its dealings with Israel. Even if the latter has gone from the south, the frontier between the two countries remains volatile: Hizbullah could go on the attack again at any time. Damascus knows it; so does Tel Aviv. The situation will last as long as the 'non peace' between the two countries persists. Clearly, Syria cannot accept too great a show on 'independence' in Lebanon until it has secured peace with Israel. ❏

Alain Gresh is editor-in-chief of Le Monde Diplomatique *in which this article first appeared.*
Translated by Wendy Kristianasen and JVH

Culture

Elfriede Jelinek

ELFRIEDE JELINEK

Viennese whirl

*E*lfriede Jelinek is
one of the most
widely read and
performed contemporary
writers in the German
language. For over 25
years, her plays and
novels have provided a
graphic and often
sardonic comment on an
Austria that has
consistently avoided
coming to terms with its
Nazi past.

As intellectuals
across Europe debated
the proper international
response to the accession
of Jörg Haider's
Freedom Party (FPÖ)
to government, Jelinek
withdrew all her plays
from the Austrian stage
and any new books
with publishers there.
She was not alone in
her gesture: actresses

Elfriede Jelinek – Credit: Serpent's Tail,

Catherine Deneuve and Sophia Loren cancelled their attendance at the Carnival
Ball and the French author Viviane Forrester instructed her publisher, Fayard,

not to sell her work to Zsolnay, the Vienna branch of the German publisher Hanser.

Vienna's own response was more divided. Ingeborg Bachmann's family has refused to allow her name to continue on the major literature prize, now renamed the Klagenfurter Literaturpreis, apparently after Haider's favourite ski resort. But the writers' and translators' Literaturhaus issued a statement saying that 'isolating not only the current government coalition, but also those forces that resist it, would mean playing into the hands of the FPÖ in its efforts to undermine voices of criticism in the population at large'. It is a cry echoed by Karl Schwarzenburg, one-time adviser to Vaclav Havel, and has been endorsed by the leader of the Viennese Jewish community, Ariel Muzicant.

Some Austrian artists are already in line for isolation. In Haider's home province of Carinthia, the avant-garde theatre group Arbos has lost its subsidy, Meina Schellander lost her public art commission, as did Cornelius Kolig, whose grandfather's murals in the Carinthian parliament were defaced by Nazi activists in the 1930s. The FPÖ claims to favour 'decent family entertainment' of a kind not provided by contemporary artists who, in the words of Haider's cultural adviser Andreas Molzer, 'behave like whores'.

Q: Why do you think the FPÖ got 27% of the vote and what do you think it intends to do, particularly where culture is concerned?

A: The election [result] was a protest against the rigid bipartite system of the Grand Coalition and the corruption of the two main parties that have governed Austria for over 30 years: the ÖVP (Catholic Party) and the SPÖ (Social Democratic Party) got their worst results since the end of the war.

Of course, there is another, darker side of all this: that of a past with which the country has never come to terms in the way Germany has. The Allied occupation in Germany was longer than in Austria and German society benefited. It was forced to develop a diversified press, and this played a major role in its democratisation. In Austria, the victims and a handful of artists and intellectuals came to terms with the past; the perpetrators and their followers were never confronted, nor were any of Austria's post-war governments.

One reason was that, in the mid-1950s, we pronounced ourselves innocent in the form of a national compact that enabled us to write our history from scratch, as it were. It's often forgotten that a disproportionate number of wartime perpetrators – and I'm talking about the most brutal accomplices to mass extermination – were native Austrians. Hitler was a fully-fledged politician and anti-Semite when he went to Germany; Eichmann was raised and educated in Austria from the age of eight; and there are innumerable other examples. The descendants of such perpetrators of atrocities as Eigruber and Murer frequently became FPÖ members, then members of parliament. Tobias Portschy was a high-ranking SS officer, a bearer of the Order of the Blood and then a member of the FPÖ until his death. The FPÖ was a known retirement retreat for old Nazis. You could find former Nazis in all Austrian political parties but the VDU [which later mutated into the FPÖ] was almost entirely made up of them.

What's clear is that our post-war disaster began with this lie we tell ourselves to hide from our history: the lie of innocence on the part of perpetrators of atrocities, lies that have run on from one generation to the next. An old Jewish man told me yesterday that the very few trials of Nazis held here illustrated how the perpetrators and their heirs knew they could get off unpunished by denigrating Jewish witnesses. As for restitution, the Social Democratic ministers were themselves guilty of recommending that proceedings be deliberately dragged out until the victims died off.

This is the bedrock of a populist like Haider, whose parents were both Nazis and never renounced those values.

I don't think Haider wants to walk in Hitler's shoes, that would be too simple. A new European fascism (which I hope never to see) would be very different from the old. The rich will try to cut themselves off from the poor – immigrants in search of work, asylum seekers and so-called 'illegals'. But, though there is still poverty in Austria, it's not the poor and destitute who voted for Haider. He's mainly supported by the nouveaux riches and petit bourgeois, who guard their prosperity jealously, and by workers who fear a fall in living standards, now blamed on 'foreigners and their low wages'. It's interesting to observe – and entirely typical of a racist party – how the FPÖ has an especially high vote in areas where there are very few foreigners. Racism and xenophobia work perfectly well without them, for they are based on fear rather than reality.

I have frequently been the victim of right-wing attacks, perhaps because I am a woman and women are, of course, not really supposed to speak out in public. Right-wing forces can only put women into the role of mother and no other. Perhaps it's also because I was once a member of the Communist Party. They even used me as a deterrent in their poster campaign, asking: 'Would you rather have Jelinek [plus a shortlist of other cultural radicals] or Art and Culture?' I am also under continual attack from the *Kronenzeitung*, which fancies itself as the guardian of 'common-sense decency' and so targets artists and anyone else of whom the editor disapproves. Nearly half the population reads it.

My decision not to have my plays performed on the Austrian stage as long as the present reactionary government was in power is a personal decision; I don't recommend everyone to emulate it. Only a reasonably well-known artist could risk making this kind of choice; at the moment I'm alone in my decision. I can't give my plays to the theatres and have them celebrated: I can't just carry on with 'business as usual', as though nothing had happened. I'm the one who suffers most because it obviously devastates my earnings. Most of my colleagues reject my position, saying: 'You only hurt those who dislike Haider anyway, and that ultimately plays into his hands.' Some are annoyed, but I'm not saying mine is the only way. Nor am I about to change my mind. Were I able to write a topical play on the current situation I might well want to see it performed, but I'm not here just to 'supply' the theatre come what may.

My new play *Macht Nichts: Eine Kleine Trilogies des Todes* (It Doesn't Matter: A Minor Death Trilogy) will be premiered by the Berliner Ensemble in the autumn. I have prohibited an Austrian premiere for the time being. The first part is about an old Nazi actress who, after death, defends the roles she played under the Third Reich. The second concerns the true, the good and the beautiful – the only real purpose of art, so reactionaries tell us. The third part is about my father, who was persecuted by the Nazis because of his race. The play happens to be highly topical. Also, I'm in the process of completing my latest novel, *Gier: Ein Unterhaltungsroman* (Greed: a popular novel), a crime novel which, among other things, deals with the new rulers and our supposedly decent, hard-working, diligent people. The protagonist is a village cop who gets women to depend on him and then kills them or makes them commit suicide in order to acquire their possessions.

I have always preferred to premiere my plays in Germany because their reception there is more matter-of-fact and causes less of an uproar.

I'm sick and tired of the slander to which I'm subjected and the emotionally charged reactions here. I can't handle them and I stay out of the way. I have been spat at on the streets and I receive endless threatening letters, many of which are also anti-Semitic.

Cultural repression will only make itself felt at a later stage, but if matters develop as in the past – even under the Social Democrats – no good will come of it. They harness the most primitive prejudices against artists and attempt to expose us as 'parasites on the healthy body of the Austrian people'. There has already been an outrageous incident in Salzburg where the FPÖ threatened to cut subsidies to any artists participating in anti-government demonstrations. In my opinion, this amounts to a restriction of our civil rights, since the right to demonstrate is incorporated into our national constitution, as is artistic freedom. Yet artists who use their freedom are persecuted and harassed by the FPÖ and its hangers-on. They want to exclude all art but 'folk art', saying the freedom that interests them is a freedom from subsidised art. If they implement this, it'll be an end to 'state artists' which is the more disgraceful because avant-garde art, which is the least secure of any, is the most dependent on public support. Contrary to what the FPÖ claim, I myself have never needed, nor received, any financial support from the state.

Q: How can people abroad show solidarity?

A: Almost everyone I know favours boycotting tourism. Tourists should take a look at the election results in the district they intend to visit and choose the places that didn't vote for the right-wing extremists. It's always possible to alter one's holiday destination and it's the sort of protest that helps us. The *Literaturhaus* has put together a list of places that voted FPÖ. I'm sure you could use them to design some attractive posters. All those communities are wealthy and depend heavily on the labour of foreign workers. They had no obvious cause to vote FPÖ, except for disillusion with our major political parties, the wish to exercise a 'negative vote', and the desire to be able to hire and fire seasonal workers and send them 'back' – whenever they feel like it. ❏

Books by **Elfriede Jelinek** *in English include* Lust, The Piano Teacher, Women as Lovers *and* Wonderful, Wonderful Times (*all from Serpent's Tail, UK).*
Interview and translation by Barbara Honrath and Amanda Hopkinson

EMILY NASRALLAH

A house not her own

The key is in her hand yet the door remains locked. The key does not find its way into the lock nor does the door respond. And for the tenth time she remembers: this is not the key to this door. It is the key that glues itself to her fingers every time she puts her hand in her purse. It is attracted to her by a magnetic power. She banishes it again.

The door opens and she hesitates for a moment before entering the apartment. She listens intently, for fear there may be someone inside. 'Someone' who does not know her, who will pounce at her and ask her who she is. Her words would trip over each other.

She stands bewildered and confused. What would she tell her interrogator? Would she say why she is here? The questioning voice would come back to her from the inside and she would remain on the doorstep, silent. She would decide not to say anything, for there are no words to explain why she is here.

'*So, why…?*' She hears the voice of the beautiful woman, emanating from the picture in the gilded frame in the centre of the salon. It screams at her and she trembles, and shivers run from her head down to her toes.

'I thought you knew,' she mutters.

The beautiful woman retreats and her voice loses its harshness. '*They told me. They wrote to me from Beirut and they told me.*'

'So they wrote…'

'*Yes, but I forgot…I thought you were another.*'

'You are right. How are you to know me, we have never met.' She hangs her head low.

★★★

This is not the first time she enters this strange apartment. She has been here for more than a week. That is, since a rocket, of a calibre she does not remember, hit her house; her beautiful house in the middle of its glorious garden in the suburb of Beirut. The rocket took it upon itself to erase all traces of her house and eradicate her garden. She can but thank the Lord that she and her family managed to escape unscathed.

A thousand thanks to God.

They had been hiding in the basement of a neighbouring building. Small houses such as hers were not built for war. Nor were the bigger houses, she muses, thinking of the sights she had witnessed on her way from the ruins of her home to the city centre. Those sights convinced her that neither palaces nor skyscrapers nor fortresses were made to withstand the might of the modern artillery being experimented with in her country. Nothing could stand up to the concentrated shelling, the random shelling, the sporadic shelling. She witnessed the incredible and said to her sorrowed soul, 'Your anguish is equal to that of others.'

She repeats the adage to herself often. Not because she feels she is above other people or her despair is more important but because, at certain points in their lives, people forget that they are but ashes and dust. There are times when they believe they are omnipotent giants, their shadows extending as far as their eyes can see. And one day they receive a blow, they know not from where, and they awaken and they look around them and they are finally aware of their time and their place.

She has lost her home. She is now in this strange dwelling that was offered to her and her family by an old friend from college. 'It is fully furnished,' the friend told her. 'The owners asked me to take care of while they're away.' Her friend gave her the key.

She is lucky. She has not ended up on the streets, nor out in the open, sleeping on the beaches like the thousands of destitute. She was lucky to have had a friend in her time of need.

★★★

She takes another step towards the living room. Instinctively she places her package on the hall table. The package tilts, it is too big for the table. The package tilts, it is too big for the table. It topples the statue of a Greek god. She rushes back to the table, rights the objet d'art, gathers her purchases and retreats to the bedroom with them, muttering apologies.

Her guilt has been constant since she set foot in the strangers' apartment, since she first attempted to open the door with the wrong key. She walks through the apartment, apologising to the tiles as she treads heavily on them. She places her possessions on a table. She hears the ghosts around her grumble. Children poke their heads out of the picture frames and shout at her, *'This is our place...You belong elsewhere.'* Their innocent smiles become ferocious, like shrapnel cut into her flesh.

And the pretty woman in the big framed picture, holding up the cascading folds of the wedding dress she wore half a century ago, runs towards her, *'What hole did you creep out of?'*

Her groom shakes his head, tugs at his bow tie and speaks softly, *'She might have lost her way. Be gentle with her. Don't frighten her.'*

Then they all shout from the walls, from behind the masks of time and dust. The voices of parents and grandparents, aunts and uncles, the living and the dead intermingle, *'Throw her out. She's a stranger. This house is not her own.'*

'You are right. All of you are right. I am only here for a short while. My house was demolished by a rocket...' But she does not continue for they have turned away and become deaf to her explanations.

She moves her things to the dressing table and is confronted by the army of bottles and jars lined up there and the souvenirs hanging on both wings of the mirror. She moves some of them to make room for her hairbrush and her few toiletries. 'Excuse us,' she murmurs. 'We are only here for a short time.' And she catches herself in her little dramatic moment and wants to laugh and cry at once. She collapses on to the nearest chair.

★★★

In her dreams, during her childhood and youth, she imagined many scenarios, drew many images for her life, but never did she imagine her present situation. She never thought, not in her wildest dreams, that she would one day take refuge in a house not her own.

She always thought the house that would hold her, and the one she loved, would be hers for ever. In childhood she had pictured it as a mud hut, on the banks of a stream among the orchards in her village. And as she grew so did her dream house. It grew taller as she grew taller. But even when it was only a tree house in her father's garden, or a tent atop their summer house, it remained special. Hers. The place where she could rest and dream, to which she could invite her friends. It remained open and welcoming.

Her words tumble and fall into the bottomless void. All that is left of her past now are words. Words and memories to be planted in the silence of this place and the emptiness of this time. She tells herself, 'We are but passers-by on this earth. No sooner do we arrive than we are carried away by wings that lift us to a place where neither our plans nor our schemes matter. A place even our imagination is powerless to describe.'

And a voice answers her, *'But people are like trees whose branches cannot grow the leaves of life unless their roots are firmly planted in the soil.'*

Ever since she had been pulled out by her roots and implanted in this new soil she has felt dizzy and numb. She holds her head in her hands, lest it, too, should fall off. Her head reels with the voice and its echo. She has to learn how to cope with a new reality.

★★★

A quarter of a century written with blood and tears, in which she built her home like a female bird builds her nest. She and he, both, against the fates. A blessed life it had been. The seeds of blessing having been planted beneath the foundations of her home, for stone and steel and wood do not make a home. Nor does luxurious furniture dictated by the fancy and whim of decorators and creative strangers. What good is it for a house to withstand the elements if the gentle breeze of love and life does not blow within? What is the meaning of a home if it is a cocoon closed to the world, and the world's dreams and magic? What is the meaning of her existence in this strange place where the walls are but stone and the doors planks of wood? And what if it were an expensive ebony? It is still only wood, and the marble is icy beneath her feet and the ceiling threatens to cave in on her.

She rises from her seat and moves aimlessly through the room and on to the balcony. There is the sea, a blue expanse, cold and remote. It reminds her of the Arctic ocean that she had once visited. And the buildings, shoulder to shoulder, hugging, each trying to hide the other's faults, the roads winding around them, grey and paved in dust. She can hear the children's cries coming at her from every direction. They hang in the air, strangely devoid of childish joy. In front of her are the balconies of neighbouring buildings, decorated with clotheslines – the trademarks of the dispossessed. She remembers that she is but a drop in this vast ocean of misery, a grain of sand on its shores. Yet she gives herself and her feelings so much importance. She wraps herself in her cloak of misery and turns this apartment into a cocoon that threatens to suffocate her. What is wrong with her? She, who even in her first home, the little village on the slopes of Mount Haramoun, had an unquenchable thirst to better herself, to learn, to rise in the world, to delve into the mysteries of the universe.

Her feet lead her around the apartment. Questions rise from deep within her, turn in an empty circle, and remain in search of answers. From which direction will her answers come?

From the West? Where the warships are anchored, spewing fire and destruction on to the land? From the North where the north winds blow icy cold, cutting into the flesh like the blade of a knife? Or from the East where the battles rage and the fronts are aflame; where explosives roar like thunder and ululating bullets write, in red and yellow fire upon the night sky, the names of those that have fallen? Or is it from the South that she will get her answers! The South!

She wraps her arms around herself as though hiding from the danger around her. Her body has become weak as a child's, left unprotected, at the mercy of the elements. She holds her body with her arms, trying to build fences around it. Then she realises that her arms are powerless to protect her battered body, for they are part of it. And the protection she so dearly desires at this moment will not come from any earthly source.

★★★

She is awakened from her deep thoughts by a fierce banging on the door. She turns around and automatically walks towards the door, not asking who it is. She reaches out to open it, then retreats. She remembers where she is. She remains in her place, fixed, listening to the banging grow louder and fiercer, beating at her like a hammer. Slowly, she withdraws to the farthest corner of the house, for she is not expecting anyone … and the house is not her own. ❏

Emily Nasrallah *is a Lebanese writer living in Beirut and Canada. She has often been censored in Lebanon for her feminist views.* A House Not Her Own *is published by gnergy books, Canada. Translation by Thuraya Khalil-Khouri*

MERSAD BERBER

War in Sarajevo

Before the wars that ripped Yugoslavia apart, Mersad Berber was renowned throughout the now divided territories and almost permanently on exhibition in in one city or another. He was almost as well known in western Europe, to which, through his training and art, he feels a natural affinity. He has not been able to exhibit in his native Bosnia since the destruction of Sarajevo, and his recent exhibition at the Albemarle Gallery in London: 'Piero della Francesca, do you remember Sarajevo?', brings together Dubrovnik Allegories, Ottoman Chronicles and Memories of Sarajevo in one place for the first time. It is a poignant reminder that this part of the world is the old 'Central Europe' and a passionate demand not to be cut out of the cultural life of western Europe today.

The work is savage, often ironic, powerfully redolent of the masters of the European renaissance he so much admires. Many of the images are etched onto what look like, and may well be, the battered pages of manuscripts destroyed in the shelling of Sarajevo's historic library. ❏

JVH

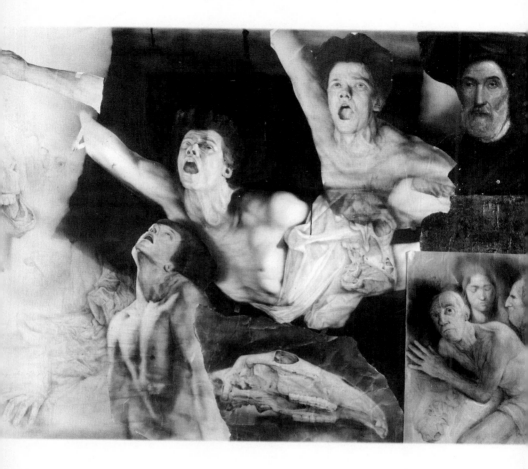

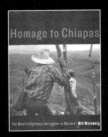

Support for

In the last year, *Index on Censorship* has been looking at ways of meeting the challenges of the future. One way in which we feel we can expand on our work is to create one single, truly International Committee of supporters, with representation from different parts of the world, to replace our individual country committees.

We want to stress how important the work of the existing country committees has been for us, and how grateful we are for their support. Without them, much of our work would not have been possible. This restructuring is merely a way of rationalising our resources. Phase 1 of International Committee is already in place and their names are shown on the inside cover of this edition. At present we are still waiting to hear back from potential representatives in other countries in Asia and the Middle East.

Again, we want to say a very big, public thank you to all the members of the country committees who have done so much for Index in the past.

Leonor Stjepic, Development Manager.

The Trustees and Directors would like to thank the many individuals and organisations who support *Index on Censorship* and Writers & Scholars Educational Trust, including:

Anonymous
The Ajahma Charitable Trust
G E Anwar
The Arts Council of England
The Bromley Trust
Clarins UK Ltd
The John S Cohen Foundation
DANIDA
Demokratifonden
The European Commission
Nicole Farhi
The Ford Foundation
The Goldberg Family Trust
The Golsoncot Foundation
The Calouste Gulbenkian Foundation
G A Hosking
Institusjonen Fritt Ord
The JM Kaplan Fund
Dr and Mrs J Matthews
Mr Raymond Modiz
Offshore

The Open Society Institute
The Onaway Trust
Pearson plc Charity Trust
Thomas Pink
Proud Galleries
CA Rodewald Charitable Settlement
Ms Ruth Rogers
The Royal Literary Fund
The Royal Ministry of Foreign Affairs, Norway
Alan and Babette Sainsbury Charitable Trust
Scottish Media Group plc
J Simpson
R C Simpson
Stephen Spender Memorial Fund
Tom Stoppard
Swedish International Development Co-operation Agency
Tiffany & Co
Ms E Twining
United News and Media plc
UNESCO
Mr and Mrs O J Whitley

Mark Thomas and guests will be performing at an Index comedy benefit in Brighton on 24th November. Details: Susannah 020 7278 2313

If you would like more information about *Index on Censorship* or would like to support our work, please contact Hugo Grieve, Fundraising Manager, on (44) 20 7278 2313 or email hugo@indexoncensorship.org

Daddy was a Nazi

All the speakers here are members of a Viennese group that brings together the children of Nazis and the children of victims of the Shoah in an effort to break the silence that conceals Austria's 'poisoned legacy' of its Nazi past from succeeding generations. The success of Jörg Haider and his right-wing nationalist party in last year's elections sowed the seeds of doubt in the Jewish members of the group, despite the fact that they had been meeting regularly since 1995

LILLY, A 50-YEAR-OLD MOTHER

I'm a Gypsy: my mother was Sinti, my father German. My mother was in concentration camps – Ravensbrück then Buchenwald – for six years. She had a vast scar on her stomach that made me think she must have been used for some kind of 'experiments'.

My father was a member of the Waffen SS. I've no idea how he and my mother met; but I do know that after the war he went down on his knees and asked her to marry him, and that she accepted, knowing that her family and her community would cut her off. It seems unthinkable, and I've always wondered how on earth she could have done it: of her 15 brothers and sisters who were taken to the camps only three survived; her baby was gassed with her parents in Auschwitz.

The marriage didn't last long: less than two years after the birth of my brother and a few months before mine my mother asked for a divorce. She left the Bavarian forest with us in tow and joined the remnants of her family on the road. We travelled in a caravan.

I lived like this until I was six ... Eventually, we set up home in Vienna so that we could go to school. My mother couldn't read herself, but she was determined that her children should have the opportunity.

The racism was relentless: it was as though the war had never happened. Gypsy children were treated like vermin; we were the lowest of the low, less than nothing.

The teacher loathed me and I was beaten regularly. I was devastated: I couldn't understand it. In spite of our poverty, we did everything in our power to look just like the other children; to be above reproach. Yet I said to myself that to be treated like this day after day, we must, at some time or other, have committed a trerrible crime. But what?

We held on to the idea that we must always be ready at any time to take off. My mother kept a tight hold on our papers and bolted her door. As for me, I had an identity problem. I was a Gypsy; and I felt 'Gypsy' despite being rejected by some Gypsies. Sure, I had fair hair and my eyes were light – but I got the blue eyes from my mother! ... My world revolved around my mother. She was a walking zombie, locked into her silence, for ever scarred by the camps. I just wanted a father.

I married an Aryan, a doctor, even though Gypsies will have nothing to do with professions that deal with blood. It was a double sacrilege: but I wanted so badly to be part of Austrian society.

My mother-in-law was still imbued with ideas from her days in the *Bund Deutscher Mädel* [Federation of German Girls] a Hitler youth organisation for girls. Her brother still denied the presence of Gypsies in the concentration camps. My mother seldom appeared at family gatherings: 'She'll die soon,' my husband used to tell me, 'then there won't be a problem.' It took years of therapy for me to find myself; to reconcile my mother and my father within me – he the executioner, she the victim – and to refuse to be a victim myself. The nature of Austrian society with its venomous silence didn't help. My mother is alive today; my husband committed suicide.

Today, Haider has made it 'respectable' for people to express their everyday, commonplace racism freely and openly. He reassures Austrians by giving voice to their unspoken fears. It's so easy to turn minorities into scapegoats for full-blooded Austrians. Oh, the arrogance of the white race! Once again, the Gypsies – like the Jews – have good reason to be afraid. Evil can rear its head again. The Austrians have found a new führer. As far as I'm concerned, Haider is the devil incarnate, the evil spirit of the forest.

YOSSI, 53-YEAR-OLD MUSICIAN

I was born in Palestine, my father having fled from the Nazi invasion of Lithuania: the Nazis killed the rest of his family. I lived in Israel until I was 16, but found the atmosphere at that time oppressive, saturated with the drama of the Shoah. The mere words 'Germany', 'Austria' were synonymous with hell. But for me, studying music, they were the birthplaces of the greatest composers. And I was worried by all this: how were these things possible? The beauty of the music, the atrocities of which I heard tell all around me: I had to go and see for myself. I was drawn to Germany.

My parests were furious. They rejected this 'Christian' music. I was torn in two by having to choose between my family and the music. I chose the music. I adored Wagner; Wagner the anti-semite! But it was the music, I thought, that spoke the truth. I got a scholarship and went to Germany. I was ecstatic. I plunged body and soul into the music. My friends never mentioned the war; I never asked questions ... I stayed for 16 years; far too long ... Then some friends in the music business mentioned Austria. It seemed like a good idea; I've been here over ten years and brought up my daughter here. A terrible mistake.

There is a deafening silence on the Nazi period; an impenetrable wall, thicker even than in Germany. There can be no contrition because nobody is to blame! Above all, let no one destroy the myth of Austria as victim! It makes me uneasy: I have difficulty in shaking the hand of any elderly Austrians. What did they do? What are they hiding? One day, in a restaurant, some elderly man at the next table smiled at me. I returned his smile without thinking. Then I was brought up short: no, I don't smile at old Nazis. Then he asked me where I came from. I said to myself, 'It's a trap. I don't tell old Nazis where I come from.' Then he said: 'I'm also a Jew...' This is just to illustrate how uncomfortable I still am in this country. It's a closed land, a place of deep secrets, old habits and clans. Even in Vienna's Jewish community. Because I'm not married to a Jew, I'm excluded from holding any office.

Today, watching the crowd I said to myself: 'They voted for Haider. They are made in his image.' Such people are dangerous ... I want those of my Austrian friends who had Nazi fathers to make their position on Haider absolutely clear. If they won't denounce him, if they show any indulgence, I'll break with them. It would demonstrate that my confidence in them is over, that our dialogue was an illusion. It would be terrible.

BIRGIT, 36-YEAR-OLD PSYCHOTHERAPIST

My father was in the Waffen SS, the Führer's elite unit. At least, that was what he told me, briefly, one day in 1976 when I had just got home from school ... People never spoke about the past; war and the pre-war years had disappeared into a black hole. Every family had its own black hole: the subject was taboo. As children, we were quick to learn not to ask questions; that this was dangerous, might even destroy the family. We were complicit in this silence: shared the responsibility in some way.

After my father died, my mother married a vicious Holocaust denier. You couldn't discuss anything with him. He denied all the Nazi atrocities, excoriated the decadence of society, the left, the Jews, homosexuals, you name it ... He voted Haider for sure, like my mother, my sister, my brother-in-law. When I go to see them, I realise I am a one-off in that group. It depresses me.

I went into therapy and, at the age of 28, finally started to find out about my father, to dig around a bit, ask questions of my mother, my uncle, my half-brothers, the military archives. The archives told me he had spent the war in Finland, the Netherlands, France. Nothing else. Most Austrian families have destroyed any documents that could compromise any of their members ... Too many things in this family have been swept under the carpet. In the country, too. Haider is putting us in touch with our lost past; maybe he's right.

ELEONORE, 45-YEAR-OLD TEACHER

My father used Nazism and the war to make his fortune. This shocked me. I don't even want to try and explain his attitude; there's nothing to understand. I feel no duty as a daughter. The rupture with my family was forced on me. That's that.

Oh yes. I spent a long time getting at the truth before this: it was scarcely ten years after my father's death that I decided to get to the bottom of things – very much against my family's wishes ... I'd always had this sense of a secret, something smouldering away, hidden under the upholstery. And when the media, as it did occasionally, invoked the Nazi atrocities, I used to imagine I had a Jewish grandmother. I badly needed to be on the other side, on the side of the victims. Besides, I was a victim of my father...

It was at the Ministry of the Interior that I learned that my father had put his factory at the service of the German government and had provided it with armaments throughout the war. He joined the Nazi Party in 1931 when it was still illegal and was one of its major funders. The factory was entirely staffed by hundreds of forced labourers. If any rebelled, my father would use the police to hunt them down. ... After serving six months in prison in 1945, he immediately recovered his factory and became an active member of the Conservative Party. He would have voted for Haider, this shallow opportunist and his party of sheep.

It's the everyday fascism that concerns me. The growing arrogance of the police who voted FPÖ [Haider's party]; the racist, anti-semitic language that was supposed to be banned but is reappearing in certain papers ... But I think the majority of Austrians are lucid enough and ready to fight.

PETER, 41-YEAR-OLD PAEDIATRICIAN

Like so many other Austrians, I, too, am the son of a Nazi. My father was from a conservative family and still at school when he joined the Nazi Party. He was enchanted by what seemed to him the idealism of the movement: its glorification of the virtues of work, of beauty, of community. The participation in something big that transcended the individual. My mother, who was German, also worked for the Hitler Youth, helping on farms. She was fascinated by this frightful Hitler.

As a medical student in Vienna, my father begged to join the Wehrmacht in Germany, then, once his studies were finished, he was sent to Russia and then France, where he was taken prisoner. On his return to Vienna he was put on trial. To pay the fine that was imposed on him, he sold the stamp collection he had inherited from his father. That's what he told me. In fact, I know very little. He was banned from medicine so became a dentist. He had two sons; I was born in 1959.

We seemed to be a modern family, like those in US films: a house, a car, money in our pockets, holidays at the beach or in the mountains.

But there was something concealed in our family. I could sense it ... It was as though my family was acting in a play; as if my parents refused themselves the right to be happy. Their lives were dedicated to work; they had no friends nor hobbies. They were locked up with their terrible secret. To whom should they talk? To whom explain with raised voices what it was that had exalted their young days. No one dared.

When they watched a film about Nazism on the TV, I noticed my parents would become increasingly tense. They never knew how to talk about it. Once my father let slip: 'That's not right! They show you the horrors, but they never talk about our ideals.' ... My father had no frame of reference for bringing up his children: no religion, no philosophy of life, no political involvement Above all, no Nazism. He didn't dare. But he pursued Jews on the TV: 'Another one! They're everywhere!' ...

It's in meeting the children of victims that I hope to discover what it is that my life lacks in some way or other. In the beginning, I was afraid: afraid of being judged, of being cast, immediately, in the role of the accused. Tagged as an executioner like my father. But the Jews in front of me were still more terrified. We have talked for a long time now, intensely, and confidence has been built. I need the group; the friendship of the other camp – the 'victims' – is precious.

There's nothing to panic about; nor to demonise. Yes, my mother was attracted to Haider. Yes, the man is somewhat fascist. Yes, our history demands that we take particular care. But Austria in the year 2000 is not the Austria of 1930! And at long last we are discussing that period! Let there be an end to the lies. ❏

An edited version of interviews first published in Le Monde, *Paris*
Translated by JVH

HUW CHRISTIE

Mbeki's mission

The enmity that exists between establishment and dissident AIDS researchers is fiercer than any other in science – only South Africa, with its ground-breaking 'truth and reconciliation' experience, could get both sides around the same table

Extraordinary political and scientific developments have been enacted this year by South Africa's Mbeki administration in the struggle for public health that is 'AIDS in Africa'. With largely sceptical reporting in the foreign and domestic media, early May saw the convening of a Presidential Panel of Inquiry into the unresolved questions of HIV/AIDS, including much of the basics of testing, epidemiology, aetiology and treatment. The *Citizen* newspaper of 4 March first reported the initiative as 'Mbeki in call to world for AIDS rethink: HIV link questioned'. The *Lancet* condemned the 'waste of time and resources re-examining issues that have been explored'. Canada's Dr Mark Wainberg, president of the powerful International AIDS Societies, suggested unorthodox AIDS scientists warrant criminal prosecution.

Mbeki's historic panel contained 33 scientists and doctors, including such luminaries as Professor Luc Montagnier, credited as co-discoverer of HIV, Dr Helene Gayle of the US CDC (Centers for Disease Control), a weighty cross-section of African doctors and other internationals, and a one-third complement of members usually referred to as 'AIDS dissidents' – Roberto Giraldo, Eleni Eleopulos, Peter Duesberg, Gordon Stewart et al (*Index* 3/98).

Almost unbelievably, after 16 years of intellectual and political hostility between these proponents of radically differing scientific views of AIDS, they met face to face in conference over a total of four days, under the attentive eye of health minister Manto Tshabalala-Msimang. The social environment of hotel breakfast, lunch and dinner provided opportunities for unprecedented introductions and informal discussions between the structured sessions, which were chaired by a Canadian professor of politics. The stated goal of the panel was to provide advice to the president on innovations in policy that would best serve the health of the people of South Africa. By the end of a further meeting in July, six weeks later, some serious outcomes had been achieved.

The key question on the agenda was: how applicable to South Africa are the received western wisdoms about HIV/AIDS?

Scientific journals were asserting in the mid-1980s that HIV was not endemic in South Africa. Now it is said to be everywhere you look: '60% of SA army may be HIV positive,' says the Johannesburg *Mail and Guardian,* based on the testing of just 33 soldiers. Other media reports suggest 'One in five teenagers' in the Jo'burg region is HIV positive. If this is 'heterosexual spread', why did it not happen in the West, where there has been no detectable increase in condom use? Why is it claimed that AIDS kills vast numbers, when there are no national figures for AIDS mortality in South Africa? Why is there no consensus on the requirements for an AIDS diagnosis? Why are the national figures for HIV positivity in South Africa extrapolated from testing in antenatal clinics with an ELISA HIV antibody test about which its manufacturer warns the principal cause of false positivity is pregnancy? What is the extent of 'false positivity' in testing, when it's well known that common African illnesses such as TB, malaria and leprosy can create positive HIV test results in the absence of HIV? When none of the illnesses now grouped as AIDS is new, what real evidence is there that a 'new' microbe is involved in the estimated increase of some of these diseases, rather than the growing stresses of poverty and malnutrition in a country of 47 million mostly rural people, many of whom are entering public health statistics for the first time?

In his welcoming address Mbeki acknowledged the criticisms he had attracted for the questions being raised and the scientifically 'broad church' of his panel.

'I've asked myself over the past few months whether the matters we've raised are folly or grace,' said Mbeki. He quoted the Irish poet Patrick Henry Pearse: 'Since the wise men have not spoken, I speak that am only a fool. A fool that have loved his folly, Yea, more than the wise men their books or their counting houses or their quiet homes, Or their fame in men's mouths ... I have squandered the splendid years that the

Lord God gave to my youth, in attempting impossible things, deeming them alone worth the toil. Was it folly or grace?'

The criticisms of Mbeki have been mostly civil in the US, UK and South African mainstream media, perhaps since the president is their preferred voice of reason in other regional issues. But commentators are clear that the president has been misled by some maverick anti-HIV 'Duesbergites' while surfing the web in the small hours in late 1999, and should dissociate himself unambiguously from 'discredited' scientists. At the World AIDS Conference held in South Africa's seaside city of Durban, a week after the second panel meeting concluded, a high-profile 'Declaration', signed by apparently thousands of researchers, and printed in *Nature*, asserted that 'there is and can be no doubt that HIV causes AIDS'. Journalists reported that Mbeki's welcoming address to the World AIDS Conference would be the perfect place to apologise, clarify and move on with the 'real world' of HIV. What the president gave in his speech, however – causing some to walk out in anger – was an emphasis on the poverty and lifestyle factors of African illnesses.

In a letter to President Clinton, Prime Minister Blair and other world leaders, leaked to and published by the *Washington Post* in May 1999, Mbeki enumerated the stretches his administration is already making to fund and support conventional anti-AIDS programmes in South Africa, including a new National AIDS Council chaired by the deputy president. But Mbeki also passionately set out some ethical concerns around his right to consult a wide variety of scientists on the issues:

'It is suggested, for instance, that there are some scientists who are "dangerous and discredited" with whom nobody, including ourselves, should communicate or interact. In an earlier period in human history, these would be heretics that would be burnt at the stake! Not long ago, in our own country, people were killed, tortured, imprisoned and prohibited from being quoted in private and in public because the established authority believed that their views were dangerous and discredited. We are now being asked to do precisely the same thing that the racist apartheid tyranny we opposed did, because, it is said, there exists a scientific view that is supported by the majority, against which dissent is prohibited.

The scientists we are supposed to put into scientific quarantine include Nobel Prize winners, members of academies of science and emeritus professors of various disciplines of medicine!

Scientists, in the name of science, are demanding that we should co-operate with them to freeze scientific discourse on HIV-AIDS at the specific point this discourse had reached in the West in 1984. People who otherwise would fight very hard to defend the critically important rights of freedom of thought and speech occupy, with regard to the HIV-AIDS issue, the frontline in the campaign of intellectual intimidation and terrorism which argues that the only freedom we have is to agree with what they decree to be established scientific truths. Some agitate for these extraordinary propositions with a religious fervour born by a degree of fanaticism which is truly frightening.'

At the time of writing, after the two plenary meetings and a faltering six-week Internet 'workshop' in between, a core of the panel is moving forward with some of the recommendations . The panel's working group on HIV testing, which includes a representative of the South African Medical Research Council, the US CDC, Australian biophysicist Eleni Eleopulos, Dr Harvey Bialy and Professor Etienne de Harven will by the end of this year, in Mbeki's words, report back 'on the reliability of and the information communicated by our current HIV tests and the improvement of our disease surveillance system'.' This will include, at last, a high-powered attempt to isolate the virus.

Virus isolation is the key stumbling block of the HIV/AIDS theory – it has never been achieved to internationally accepted standards. Until the mid-1970s, virus isolation meant separating virus particles from everything in the cell culture that is not virus. It's then not very taxing to analyse the particles' proteins and genetic material, and test for infectivity. It's a careful process, because all experts agree that there are abundant particles in nature and in cell cultures that in many respects resemble viruses, but are not.

With HIV, this process has never been fulfilled – not even from patients with sky-high 'viral load'. Indirect or surrogate markers, all of which are non-specific, have had to be accepted for 15 years. But virus isolation is the only gold standard to evaluate the efficiency or otherwise of indirect HIV tests – right now the ELISA, the Western Blot, the PCR all measure indirect markers.

Manufacturers know this. The most commonly used HIV test, the

ELISA, has a package-mounted warning: 'At present there is no recognised standard for establishing the presence or absence of antibodies to HIV-1 and HIV-2 in human blood.' For the PCR: 'The Amplicor HIV-1 Monitor test is not intended to be used as a screening test for HIV or as a diagnostic test to confirm the presence of HIV infection.'

By Christmas, and with the expenditure of a significant budget, the South African government will have its own hard data on whether there can be any scientific proof for the existence of a novel exogenous virus in the community. Depending on the outcome of the first set of experiments, so the role of further research will become clear.

In an interview with British journalist Joan Shenton, Mbeki revealed a sense of urgency: 'And the matter is critical because the reason we are doing all of this is to be able to respond correctly to what is reported to be a major catastrophe on the African continent. We have to respond correctly, and urgently, and you can't respond correctly by closing your eyes and ears to any point of view, any scientific evidence that is produced. A matter that seems to be very clear, in terms of the alternative view that is being presented, is what do you expect to happen in Africa with regard to immune systems, where people are poor, subjected to repeated infection, and all of that? Surely you would expect these immune systems would collapse, and I've no doubt that that is happening. But then to attribute such immune deficiency to a virus produces a specific response, and what we are discussing here, as the South African government, is that it seems incorrect to respond to this AIDS challenge within a narrow band. If we only said there's a virus – safe sex, use a condom, end of story, we won't stop the spread of AIDS in this country.' ❏

Huw Christie is the editor of Continuum, *the magazine dedicated to providing better understanding of HIV/AIDS. More at www.continuummagazine.org*